EXPLORING
THE THAMES
WILDERNESS

Published by Adlard Coles Nautical
an imprint of Bloomsbury Publishing Plc
50 Bedford Square, London WC1B 3DP
www.adlardcoles.com

First published by Adlard Coles Nautical in 2013

ISBN 978-1-4081-8112-6
ePDF 978-1-4081-8113-3
ePub 978-1-4081-8114-0

A CIP catalogue record for this book is available from the British Library.

This book is produced using paper that is made from wood grown
in managed, sustainable forests. It is natural, renewable and
recyclable. The logging and manufacturing processes conform to the
environmental regulations of the country of origin.

Typeset in The Sans and American Typewriter.
Printed and bound in China by C&C Offset Printing, Ltd.

Commissioned by Elizabeth Multon
Edited by Jenny Clark
Design by Nicola Liddiard
Maps by John Plumer

Every reasonable effort has been made to ensure that the content in
this book is complete and accurate at the time of going to press, but
the authors and publisher disclaim any responsibility for any errors or
omissions, and disclaim any warranty or liability for actions taken (or not
taken) on the basis of information contained herein.

EXPLORING
THE THAMES
WILDERNESS

A guide to the natural Thames

RICHARD MAYON-WHITE & WENDY YORKE
ON BEHALF OF THE RIVER THAMES SOCIETY
AND THE THAMES RIVERS TRUST

ADLARD COLES NAUTICAL

BLOOMSBURY
LONDON · NEW DELHI · NEW YORK · SYDNEY

Contents

5 Culham to Tilehurst ... p82

6 Reading to Maidenhead ... p104

Foreshore at Limehouse

Reedbeds at Waterhay

Grid references to Ordnance Survey maps are given in square brackets, for example [SU017938].

We have done our best to get up-to-date website addresses. Some will change with time and we recommend checking our website www.thameswilderness.org.uk where we may have listed an alternative.

All photographs in the book were taken by the authors on their visits to the places described.

Acknowledgements

The River Thames Society was founded in 1962 to protect the natural beauty of the Thames, adjacent lands and buildings of historic interest, and to promote nature conservation. Its members are among all those who value this living heritage, from source to sea. The Society supports and contributes to the efforts of other organisations that have similar interests in the river, and aims to preserve and extend amenities and encourage the use of the river for many different purposes. It also appoints river wardens, who work to keep the river healthy so that everyone can enjoy it. In short, the River Thames Society is the independent voice of the river.

The Thames Rivers Trust is an environmental charity dedicated to restoring the Thames and its tributaries to benefit people and wildlife. The Trust was first established in 1986, as the Thames Salmon Trust, which successfully installed fish passes on the upper Thames and River Kennet. In 2005, a wider catchment approach led to the charity being renamed the Thames Rivers Restoration Trust, and in 2012 it became the Thames Rivers Trust. The Trust works in partnership with many other conservation organisations to deliver river restoration and public education projects that contribute to achieving good water quality in all rivers throughout the Thames Catchment.

We are grateful to Thames Water and Wilderness Expertise for sponsoring the Thames Wilderness project. Their help came at a critical moment, making the project possible and ensuring that the book and the website look so attractive. Numerous individuals have given their help. The river wardens started the project, and the members of the River Thames Society and the Trustees of the Thames Rivers Trust have been most supportive. In addition, the managers of the various reserves have been founts of knowledge and enthusiasm. We were always made to feel welcome when we visited the reserves, and had wonderful chats about wildlife with the many people we met on our explorations.

We thank our family and friends for kindly sharing, or at least tolerating, our enthusiasm for this Thames guide and our love of the natural river environment. We give a special acknowledgement to Valerie Mayon-White who helped with the Thames Wilderness Project up to her death in October 2011. Port Meadow was her favourite place.

Thames Rivers Trust

Restoring the Thames for people and wildlife

*Tower Bridge – the epitome
of Thames heritage*

1. The Thames ~ our living heritage

The perfect start to the day: Port Meadow, Oxford, on a winter morning. Early sunlight shines across the lake in the middle of the meadow, making the plumage on the widgeon glow with warm colours, contrasting with the nip of an easterly wind. The ducks talk to one another with piping calls, while geese give their haunting honk as they fly in to graze. The swans look elegant, as they always do. Across the meadow, the Thames makes its curving course from the Cotswolds on its way to the East Coast. Here you are connected with nature.

Ducks on Port Meadow at dawn

The River Thames has been the inspiration for many creative activities – painting, poetry, music, stories, photography – and this book is but one small example. It began as a project – an idea that emanated from the wardens of the River Thames Society – to describe the wildlife habitats along the Thames. Each warden looks after a reach of the river, and thus learns its charms and peculiarities. Combining the wardens' knowledge was a great start in listing the nature reserves along the Thames, with a view to sharing the information with others. We have chosen places that are managed to provide wildlife habitats, are open to the public, and lie within a mile of the river. We have made a point of including sites that are little known, but that have special natural features for you to discover and explore for yourselves.

The 'greening' of the Thames

The idea of 'green spaces' is that they should be places where plants and animals can survive naturally, protected from unsuitable development. The Thames is attractive to wildlife because it provides an open green corridor that runs right across southern England, much of which is densely populated. The flood meadows described in this book were originally valuable grazing land, and were never suitable for streets and houses. It is only recently though that we have understood their importance as sponges to hold floodwater, and it is our good fortune that the river has forced us to keep so much of its banks covered with plants instead of concrete, leaving wide open spaces beside the Thames, above and below London. Plants and animals need this green corridor to live, breed, travel and survive, and of course this means that humans can then enjoy their presence and the contribution they make.

People talk of 'wilderness', but what does this actually mean? Often the term is used to mean land that has never been cultivated or managed by humans. However, there is very little land on the planet that has not been affected in one way or another by human activity, so it is reasonable to broaden its definition to include places that are conserved to allow wildlife, both plants and animals, to thrive. In England today, conservation requires active management, which is why many of the places in this book are owned by wildlife trusts and similar organisations.

Like the river that defines it, this conserved land is continually changing in detail while remaining essentially the same. Much of the land has been recovered from derelict industry, and is now protected against inappropriate development. Gravel extraction has affected the Thames from the Cotswolds to the Estuary, and it has left a chain of lakes, from Swillbrook Lakes to Cliffe Pools, for water sports, fishing and water birds. Reeds and willows have grown quickly to soften the edges of the lakes, while brambles, hawthorn bushes and nettles make safe havens for small creatures. Leaving some land as islands in these lakes protects nesting birds and makes the waterscape more interesting.

As well as past industries, modern businesses can also provide opportunities for wildlife. The huge numbers of people living and working in the Thames Valley and London depend on the river for their water supply, which of course requires large reservoirs. With sympathetic management, these reservoirs can be made attractive to wildlife. Farmoor Reservoir is one such example, with the added bonus of the ponds and bird hides at Pinkhill and Shrike Meadows. In west London, the Leg O'Mutton Nature Reserve shows what can be done with a reservoir when it is no longer needed to store water for human use. The need for clean drinking water has resulted in the Thames becoming progressively less contaminated by human waste and chemicals, and this of course benefits wildlife. However, as the climate changes there is a danger that increasing demand will result in the extraction of too much water from the tributaries, adversely affecting the tributaries themselves and their wildlife – hence the need for continuing conservation.

The human needs for energy and heat (in the form of gas, oil and electricity) have greatly altered parts of the Thames, most prominently by the refineries and power stations beside the Estuary. A century ago, most towns had their

> *The need for clean drinking water has resulted in the Thames becoming progressively less contaminated by human waste and chemicals.*

Greylag geese, fishermen and sailors on Farmoor Reservoir

own gas works and power stations, and although these industries had unattractive features, some of the former sites have now become wildlife habitats. The peregrine falcon roosts on Bankside Power Station in London, and the Thames Valley Park Nature Reserve in Reading is impressive. For safety, oil refineries are surrounded by wide spaces, and the result of this on Canvey Island is the large RSPB West Canvey Reserve and its adjacent land. The high chimneys of power stations on the Isle of Grain and the cooling towers at Didcot are conspicuous reminders of human needs, but they can help to make us more appreciative of the wilderness areas that do remain along the Thames.

The sense of space is part of the attraction of large rivers like the Thames; its flood meadows and marshes – too many to name in this introduction – add to the expanse. This appreciation is heightened by the hills offering stunning views, from Wytham Wood, Wittenham Clumps, Hartslock Meadow, Richmond and Greenwich Parks, to Northward Hill in Kent. Small is beautiful too, and there is much to be found by looking down and focussing on the detail – individual flowers for example. The small reserves are valued as links in the chain, and are certainly worth exploring for plants, animals, insects, spiders and snails. Common species are as important as the rarities.

Some of the reserves on islands are easy to reach and open at all times.

Islands evoke a special sense of adventure. Some of the reserves on islands are easy to reach and are open at all times: Aston's Eyot in Oxford; View Island in Reading; and the Swale Reserve on the Isle of Harty. Others are not so

Mallard, common but handsome!

accessible: Chiswick Eyot can only be reached at low tide; and Isleworth Ait requires special permission. These restrictions are there for a good reason: they protect the wildlife.

May we enter?

The River Thames Society and the Thames Rivers Trust share the aim of improving public use of the Thames, and the purpose of this book (and the project of which it is part) is to help you find and enjoy the wildlife habitats along the river. In deciding which places to include, access was a key factor. The Thames Path and many reserves are open at all times. Some reserves are open from dawn to dusk, with shorter opening hours in winter than summer. Some have car parks that shut at 5pm, even though the reserve itself remains open. A few places have limited opening times. Wherever you go, check the opening dates and times first.

It is worth noting that public access usually refers to those on foot. Dogs are not permitted on some reserves, and must be kept on a lead in others because they would disturb the animals or birds. Horse riders and cyclists should keep to designated paths. Mooring at the banks of the river is restricted to places permitted by the landowner, who is entitled to charge a fee. Please take heed of notices about dogs, cycling, parking and mooring, as we do not want access to be lost because of misuse.

Visiting on foot or by boat is the ideal way to enjoy a wilderness like the Thames, because you have time to look around and take in the beauty of the environment. However, it isn't always possible to take the leisurely approach, so we've also given information on car parks, public transport and cycle routes. If the way to a place is well signposted, we have only written a few directions. If the way isn't so obvious, we've given more detail. The Ordnance Survey map (grid) references are generally to one of the entrances. If we know of a useful postcode, we have included it in the directions, but many of the places do not have postal addresses.

Please use the information given on the project's website (www.thameswilderness.org. uk) and that provided by the managers of the individual reserves on their websites and in their booklets.

How much time you allow for your visit will obviously depend on the size of the reserve and your particular interests. You may be making a very short visit as you walk, cycle or travel by boat past the reserve. Alternatively, you may plan a whole day with a picnic. Or you may even want a much lengthier involvement as a volunteer, giving you the opportunity to help with maintenance, to monitor species, and to get to know a particular reserve very well. Volunteering opportunties and contact details are provided for you in the 'Get Involved' section of Chapter 12.

Wilderness is boundless

When compiling this book, we started with the rule that all the reserves should be within a mile of the Thames 'as the crow flies'. We wanted to include all the places within easy

Sanderling dodging the waves at Southend

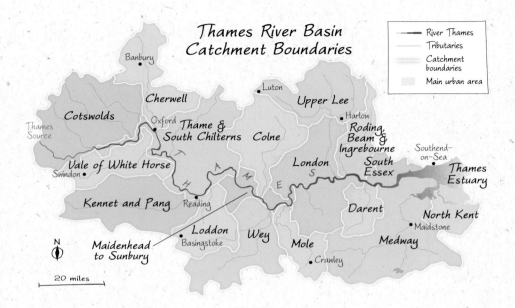

Thames River Basin Catchment Boundaries

Legend:
— River Thames
Tributaries
Catchment boundaries
Main urban area

Banbury
Cherwell
Cotswolds
Luton
Upper Lee
Thames Source
Oxford
Thame & South Chilterns
Colne
Harlow
Roding, Beam & Ingrebourne
Southend-on-Sea
Vale of White Horse
Swindon
London
South Essex
Thames Estuary
Kennet and Pang
Reading
Darent
North Kent
Maidstone
Loddon
Basingstoke
Wey
Mole
Medway
Maidenhead to Sunbury
Crawley
N
20 miles

walking distance of the main river. To the wildlife, the tributaries and backwaters are just as attractive as the main river, so we have allowed ourselves to go a little further from the Thames in some places. In the future, we plan to explore all the tributaries until we have a complete picture of the Thames River Basin.

The Thames River Basin is known as the Thames Catchment because it includes all the land that drains into the main river. Water flows into the Thames from the 38 tributaries, draining at least 18 major river catchments.

Geology

The geology of the Thames tells a story of wide-ranging variety, arising in the limestone hills of the Cotswolds and flowing through clay and chalk before it reaches the sea. The limestone gives the water a hardness (calcium carbonate) that is familiar to everyone who has tapwater from the Thames. From the Cotswolds, the Thames flows through Oxford

Clay that is the foundation of the upper Thames floodplain. Amid the clay are large deposits of limestone gravel left by glaciers during the ice ages. At Oxford, the Thames twists through a ridge of Corallian limestone to run through more clays to reach the chalk of the Chiltern hills. The chalk streams from Goring to Maidenhead add more calcium carbonate, before the Thames flows through

Beech woodland at Medmenham – a typical habitat of chalk soil

London Clay to Teddington. The Thames becomes a tidal river at Teddington, with increasing concentrations of salt as it approaches the sea.

As a result of its unique geology, the Thames hosts a number of significant wildlife habitats – in many cases protected for the species that breed there and which you can read about in this book. Importantly, these are chalk streams, lowland herb-rich hay meadows, wet heath land and mires, bog, woodland, saltmarshes, wildflower meadows, reedbeds and alder woodland on the floodplains.

The Thames' social history

The river's social history can be traced through its trading and transport past. The movement of goods changed from horse-drawn barges through steam-boats and railways to modern container ships and motorways. Ferries and fords have been replaced by bridges.

The ecological history of the Thames has ebbed and flowed from glory to decline and back again over the years, just as the river itself winds its way across the land. Although the Thames won an international prize in 2010 for being one of the cleanest metropolitan rivers in the world, this does not tell the whole story. In this book we hope to show you how you too can play a role in looking after the River Thames, at the same time as enjoying its many fascinating features and discovering all the adventures it has to offer.

Evidence of human habitation along the Thames goes back to Neolithic times, and there are Bronze Age burial mounds at Port Meadow (Oxford) and Cock Marsh (Cookham). The Romans built a bridge and trading centre where the City of London stands today. The Saxons established many of the river's traditional uses for farming, fishing, milling, travelling and trading, at places such as Goring and Reading as well as London. The Thames and its many activities were recorded in the Doomsday Book. The Magna Carta was signed by King John in AD 1215 at Runnymede on the Thames, and Samuel Pepys wrote about the Thames in his

Traditional boats preserve the history of the Thames

famous diaries as he recorded the Plague and Great Fire of London in the 1660s.

The Tudor and Stuart monarchs enjoyed the river and its pageantry, building palaces at Hampton Court, Kew, Richmond, Whitehall and Greenwich, and in 1607 the first Frost Fair was held on the frozen Thames. During the 16th and 17th centuries the City of London expanded with the growth in world trade. New docks were built to increase the space to handle cargoes, with names that survive as reminders of their trades, and in the 18th century the Thames was one of the world's most active trading waterways. In the 19th century, the river stopped freezing each winter, and a new London Bridge was opened in 1831, with the wider arches allowing large boats to pass upstream.

In Victorian times the river suffered badly from the effects of trade expansion, population growth and industrial development. This reached a nadir during the 'Great Stink' of 1858, when the foul smell of untreated sewage actually caused a sitting of the House of Commons to be abandoned. However, the sewage drainage system for London designed by Sir Joseph Bazalgette in the 1860s solved the problem for the next century. With the growth

Jubilee River

of the railways, the use of the river for transport was reduced, but recreational and sporting activities expanded – with annual rowing regattas, sailing events, riverside fairs and other public events.

The Thames has long been used for fishing, especially eel trapping, and until the 19th century it was one of the best salmon rivers in England. Fishing on the non-tidal river is now only for sport, but in the estuary it is (just) economically viable. In the past the trees were harvested for building houses and ships, for firewood and for basket-making; other trading activities included watermills for flour and paper production and for metal beating. By the 19th century, the main port activities had moved eastwards from central London to the Docklands. Upstream, housing began to replace riverside businesses, bridges replaced ferries, and hard roads replaced muddy tracks. The loss of agricultural land and the expansion of towns has of course continued to affect the River Thames and its tributaries up to the present day.

Ecological river revival

The Thames has always been a focus of public celebration and the Thames Diamond Jubilee Pageant in June 2012 bore witness to the central place that the Thames has in the heart of Britain. The exhibition 'Royal River: Power, Pageantry and the Thames' was another celebration in the summer of 2012, showing the river's historic legacy and ensuring that future generations understand the

Symbol of maritime heritage at Thurrock Thameside Nature Park

significance of the Thames. This was staged at the National Maritime Museum at Greenwich on the occasion of her Majesty the Queen's Diamond Jubilee and attracted thousands of people to look at, and think about, the Thames in new ways.

Intertwined with the cultural and historical glories of Britain (illustrated by these major public events and other activities on the shores of the Thames) there have been bleak periods when the river has suffered badly. The pressures of rural decline, urban sprawl, industry and transport needs, the arrival of the railways, riverbed modifications, population growth, trade expansion, globalisation, intensive farming practices and commercial development have all taken their toll on one of our most valuable natural resources.

The ecological history of the Thames has ebbed and flowed from glory to decline and back again over the years.

In 1957, the Thames was a heavily polluted river incapable of supporting life and was declared biologically dead by the London Natural History Museum. Yet in 2010, the

Thames won the world's largest environmental river management prize, the Theiss Riverprize, at the 13th International River Symposium in Perth, Western Australia. This award recognised the dramatic recovery of the Thames to a thriving ecosystem, supporting more than 125 different fish species – including salmon and sea trout – and this abundance of fish has even attracted otters back to the Thames. This dramatic improvement was attributed to the restoration of more than 44 miles of river and 400 habitats. The award, received by the Environment Agency and the Thames Rivers Restoration Trust, recognised the dedicated work of thousands of people in many private and public organisations. It also celebrated the work by industries, farmers, water companies and other businesses to reduce pollution and improve water quality. These measures in combination were hailed as bringing the River Thames back to life.

It is critical that we keep up this good work. We are the custodians of nature, and it is up to us to ensure that the river remains healthy for future generations. The River Thames provides two-thirds of London's drinking water, and although water quality has been much improved, there are still significant challenges being faced. The current pressures on our river systems include:

• physical modification of the water channels;
• diffuse pollution from agriculture and urban sources;
• abstraction and high demand for water;
• the dramatic effects of climate change and drier conditions;
• invasive non-native plant and animal species;
• a growing human population in southeast England;
• point source pollution from sewage works;
• ageing infrastructures.

But there is much good work being done across the Thames Catchment to mitigate these challenges. New projects by the Rivers Trusts, Wildlife Trusts, Environment Agency, Natural England, Thames Water Company, Port of London Authority, and the many volunteer groups mentioned in this book, are combining to preserve and increase understanding about the value and need to protect rivers and wetlands, water quality, wildlife habitats, access and recreational opportunities.

There have been significant conservation improvements successfully introduced and implemented during the last 50 years. The Jubilee River Flood Alleviation Scheme between Maidenhead and Windsor, completed in 2002, created a 7 mile stretch of artificial river as a flood relief channel with re-created natural habitats. This provides flood protection to more than 10,000 homes in Windsor and Maidenhead.

Thames Conservancy sign – a mark of history

The innovative Thames Flood Barrier in east London, completed in 1982, protects London from the risk of flooding as a result of high tides and strong winds from the North Sea. This creative engineering achievement was prompted by the severe floods of 1955, when 300 people were drowned and more than 160,000 acres of farmland were flooded. Flooding has been a long-term problem in the Thames Catchment, and other significantly damaging floods were recorded in 1928, 1947, 1953 and 2007.

The Thames Barrier

The Thames Estuary is highly dynamic, and its channels, sandbanks and mudflats are continually shifting. They produce suspended sediments, often giving the river a muddy and rather grubby appearance that hides its improving quality.

Other effective river restoration work being completed in recent years includes the launch of the London Rivers Action Plan in 2009, set up to co-ordinate the management of over 58 new river restoration projects. Thames Estuary 2100 is a 100 year plan addressing the management of tidal flood risk in the Thames Estuary, to protect more than 1.25 million people and £200 billion worth of property. The Thames Tunnel Project is intended to reduce the 39 million tonnes of untreated sewage from storm drains that overflow into the tidal Thames every year from Bazelgette's overloaded Victorian system. Britain's first climate change park, opened to the public in May 2012, has been created at Mayesbrook in northeast London.

An unfortunate effect of making the Thames a better wildlife habitat is the invasion by non-native species. These threaten the natural wildlife and flourish because they have no natural predators or ecologically limiting factors. Zebra mussels, Asiatic clams, signal crayfish and Chinese mitten crabs probably arrived in the ballast water of international shipping long ago. The mitten crab, in particular, endangers our own native crabs in the Thames by competing for food and space, and they are also causing structural damage by undermining the riverbanks. Mink that escaped from fur farms in past years hunted the native water vole ('Ratty' in Wind in the Willows) close to extinction. There are also increasingly large numbers of invasive plants such as Japanese knotweed, giant hogweed, floating pennywort and Himalayan balsam. They compete for light, and steal sparse nutrients needed by the local wildflowers and native trees to survive.

On the plus side, farmers are reducing the run-off of fertilisers and pesticides from fields to streams, fencing cattle away from riverbanks, and improving farming practices. Armies of community and corporate volunteers clean up litter and remove rubbish from the rivers and riverbanks. Others are educating people about the benefit and value of river systems and teaching us all how to take care of them. Innovative citizen science programmes are being introduced, giving the public new opportunities to learn about life in the river and to volunteer for flora and fauna species monitoring programmes. There are new projects to transform the many miles of concrete channels back to naturally meandering rivers, to create new natural reserves, and to improve wildlife habitats – increasing fish migrations upstream and encouraging returning species. These efforts are making the River Thames a truly living river again.

People say that the Thames is a place where they find a sense of peace and quiet. We hope that this book will be helpful in giving you information about places to visit and the wonders of nature that you will discover there. We can all share our natural heritage with our native wildlife, and we can look after it for the enjoyment of present and future generations. Whenever we are beside the Thames, we think how lucky we are to be able to reach the open spaces and appreciate the valuable wildlife. This book is aimed at sharing this love of the Thames, and its sense of adventure and wilderness.

Himalayan balsam and Canada geese are two common non-native species

Memorial seat in Quarry Wood with a splendid view over Bisham and Marlow

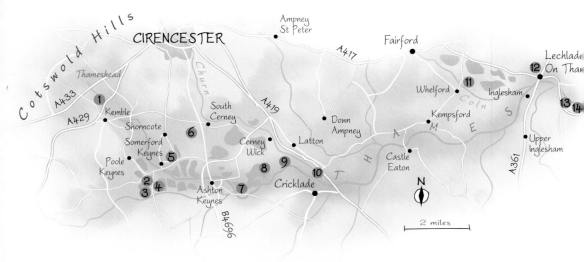

2. The Cotswolds: Kemble to Buscot

The charm of exploring the wildlife habitats along the Thames is that you get to discover some truly lovely and interesting places, none more so than the Cotswolds where the Thames begins its long journey to the sea. From here, the Thames Path accompanies the river for 192 miles as far as Erith in east London. The path is a green corridor that can be considered to be a nature reserve, because it is managed with wildlife in mind. It gives the public access to the river's edge for much of its length, except where landowners have refused permission for a path along their part of the riverbank. Fortunately, the wildlife does not have to obey the law!

There were proposals in the 1950s that the Thames should be one of the newly established National Parks, which would have made it easier to protect the public access that has to be fought for every time a riverside development is planned. Unfortunately, the Thames did not become a National Park and it took 40 years for the Thames Path to be adopted as a National Trail, creating a continuous public route from the source to the Thames Barrier. Now the Thames Path continues beyond the Thames Barrier towards the sea, becoming the Saxon Shore Way along the North Kent Coast. Eventually there will be a Thames Estuary Coastal Path that runs on both sides of the Thames, linking with the Thames Path and all the reserves that we describe in this book.

Marsh orchid at Clattinger Farm

The infant Thames at Kemble on a frosty morning

1 Kemble and Thameshead

▶ HOW TO GET THERE

The source [ST981993] and the A429 bridge over the Thames [ST 991979]

The A429 bridge over the Thames north of Kemble is about a mile north of the centre of Kemble, and there is usually space to park a car. From the bridge, follow the Thames Path signs in a westerly direction. After two fields, you will cross the A433 and continue across two more fields to the source at the edge of a wood. Trains from Swindon to Stroud stop at Kemble Station, as do buses between Cirencester and Tetbury.

A stone and signpost mark the source of the Thames and the start of the Thames Path. Although it is in a pleasant rural setting on the edge of a wood, the designated source can be disappointing. It is often dry with no signs of a spring or stream. A footpath reaches the source across two fields from the A433 road (the Fosse Way). As there are no parking places on the A433, we recommend starting near Kemble, which has a railway station and bus services. On the A429 road on the northern edge of Kemble, there is a bridge with space to park and a helpful information board. Here the course of the river can be seen easily, even when there is no water flowing. This is about 2 miles from the official source, which can be found by following the Thames Path signs in a northwesterly direction. Looking at the riverbed, you will see some reeds and other water-loving plants even when there is no stream. If there has been a lot of rain, you are likely to find a group of springs and a stream – evidence that you have discovered the beginning of the Thames! A walk through the fields and across the A433 will bring you to the starting point of the Thames Path. If the river is dry at the bridge near Kemble, you can explore the Thames Path to the east until you find running water. Listen for larks on a fine day, or watch the rooks cavorting across a windy sky.

2 Lower Moor Farm

The first nature reserve along the Thames, where water is always present, is at Lower Moor Farm. Here you will find a group of lakes, ponds and streams mixed with woodland, hedges and meadows. The lakes were formed from gravel pits dug in the 1970s, which are now conserved with reedbeds and islands. There is a teaching centre, with lots of information and displays of plants and pictures of wildlife. Toilets are available when the centre is open.

The lakes are a constant source of food for birds; ducks and swans reach down for weeds, grebes and cormorants dive for fish, and swallows and martins swoop over the water, catching insects in summer. There is a choice of walks; a short one from the car park to a bird hide by Cottage Lake and onto the path by Mallard Lake (suitable for wheelchairs), or a longer walk across Flagham Brook, passing a second bird hide overlooking Swallow Pool, to the Sandpool Reserve that also has a bird hide overlooking a pond. A path continues around the top of Swallow Pool, leading back to the car park (about 1 mile). Longer walks can be taken to the beautiful wildflower meadows at Clattinger Farm. Swillbrook Lakes (see page 29) are on the far side of a lane on the east side of Clattinger Farm (see page 28).

HOW TO GET THERE

Lower Moor Farm [SU007938]

Lower Moor Farm is on the western edge of the Cotswold Water Park. The entrance is on Spine Road (west) between Somerford Keynes and Oaksey, and the car park is close to the teaching centre. If you are using the Thames Path, walk westwards from the Neigh Bridge Country Park picnic area [SU018946] beside the Spine Road for a mile to reach the entrance. There are good cycle paths around the Cotswold Water Park and Lower Moor Farm is reached by minor roads.

www.wiltshirewildlife.org/Reserves/lowermoorfarm.htm

Teaching room at Lower Moor Farm, made with traditional materials

Clattinger Farm

3 Clattinger Farm

Clattinger Farm is a group of wildflower meadows that lie between Swillbrook Lakes and Lower Moor Farm. It is at its best in late spring and early summer, when there are many marsh orchids and some bee orchids among the buttercups and ox-eye daisies. At other times of year it is a pleasant grassland space. The meadows have never had artificial fertilisers and survived because they were never sold for gravel extraction – a splendid example of conservation.

HOW TO GET THERE

Clattinger Farm [SU017938]

Clattinger Farm can be visited at the same time as Lower Moor Farm. At Lower Moor, use the information board to choose your way to the meadows of Clattinger Farm. Alternatively, you can walk directly into the meadows from Minety Lane opposite the Swillbrook Lakes. On the Spine Road (west) in Cotswold Water Park, turn south at a crossroads at the Neigh Bridge Country Park, into Minety Lane. After half a mile, there is a small parking place with a gated footpath to Lower Moor, and a stile and footpath into Clattinger Farm.

Common blue damselfly

4 Swillbrook Lakes

Swillbrook Lakes are popular with birdwatchers, who look and listen for warblers, nightingales, sand martins and swallows. By May the sedge warbler's song is fighting for attention amid the songs of the reed warbler, blackcap and willow warbler. Great crested grebes, coots and mallard nest around the lakes.

In summer, the dragonflies and damselflies appear; the lakes are home to 13 species. The bright common blue damselfly is one of the most numerous of these delicate insects. You will also see the blue-tailed and emerald damselflies. At the end of summer, hobbies (small falcons) gather to feast on dragonflies, sand martins and swallows.

The path by the lakes was changed in 2012, to be further away from the houses in the Lower Mill Estate. If you follow the path you will reach a lake, Flagham Fen, where beavers are being reintroduced to Britain. The beavers are fenced in, so they may not meet a strict definition of 'wildlife', but they represent an interesting project. The footpath continues along a meadow beside the Swillbrook stream which the Lower Mill Estate has called the 'otter corridor'.

Across the lane at the entrance to Swillbrook Lakes are a stile and footpath into Clattinger Farm meadows, and another path through a gate that goes directly to Lower Moor Farm.

HOW TO GET THERE

Swillbrook Lakes [SU017938]

From the B4696 South Cerney/Ashton Keynes road in the Cotswold Water Park, take Spine Road running west to Minety Lane, near Somerford Keynes. Turn south for about half a mile. There is parking space in the gateways on either side of the road. The Swillbrook Lakes Nature Reserve and information board are on the east side of the road. The Thames Path runs by the turning from the Spine Road into Minety Lane.

Swillbrook Lakes

▶ HOW TO GET THERE

Coke's Pit [SU015950]

Coke's Pit is on the east side of Somerford Keynes in the Cotswold Water Park, just north of the Spine Road (west) and near to the Watermark Cotswold Country Park and Beach (formerly called Keynes Country Park). There is no car park at the reserve, but parking is possible in Somerford Keynes and the Country Park. There is a place to hire cycles near the reserve and a cycle path beside the Spine Road. It is half a mile from the Thames Path.

www.waterpark.org/leisure/cokes_pit_lnr.html

5 Coke's Pit

Coke's Pit was excavated 40 years ago and was given to the Cotswold Park Trust in 2002. After some improvements to the wildlife areas it became a Local Nature Reserve – the first in the Water Park. Coke's Pit is home to many breeding birds, including reed bunting, tufted duck, nightingale and great crested grebe. The mammals there include water vole and water shrew, and there are vast numbers of dragonflies, and also the lesser bearded stonewort, an alga-like plant. Improvements include information boards around Coke's Pit, artificial tern rafts in the lake, and a bird hide only a few yards from the road. It is a popular fishing lake, noted for its carp. There is plenty of family entertainment for the children at the Cotswold Country Park and Beach.

Coke's Pit Lake

View from the bird hide at Shorncote

6 Shorncote Reedbeds

Shorncote Reedbeds are a small reserve on the northern side of the Cotswold Water Park, a mile to the west of South Cerney. Gravel is still being extracted in this area, but Shorncote was the first quarry in the Water Park to be restored for wildlife. Bittern, reed bunting, water rail and reed warbler are among the birds recorded in the reedbeds around the small lakes. There are water voles in residence and otters have been seen.

Beside the path from South Cerney is a wildflower meadow. This path continues past the reedbeds and bird hides, through the quarries, to skirt the northern edge of the Cotswold Country Park.

A playground is located near the car park in South Cerney, where there are shops and a pub.

 HOW TO GET THERE

Shorncote Reedbeds [SU033967]

If coming by car, park at South Cerney, walk across the playing fields, cross the road, and follow a good path to the bird hides. Or you can park at the Cotswold Country Park and Beach (see Coke's Pit) and walk along paths from there. The Thames Path is about 2 miles away, via a path that winds around the north of Somerford Keynes. South Cerney is on a bus route from Swindon to Cirencester.

www.waterpark.org

7 Waterhay

⊙ HOW TO GET THERE

**Waterhay [SU060933] and
Cleveland Lakes [SU075947]**

There is a car park and
information board at
Waterhay Bridge along the
road between Cricklade and
Ashton Keynes. It is a short
distance from the car park to
the Thames Path. Cleveland
Lakes are close to National
Cycle Network Route 45 and
are a short diversion from the
Thames Path. See the circular
walk on pages 36-37 for more
details.

www.waterpark.org

Waterhay, near Cricklade, is the first reserve immediately beside
the Thames Path if travelling from the source. It has a bird hide
that used to overlook a lake, with a variety of birds to watch. The
lake was used as a lagoon to settle sand and mud from water
circulating around the other lakes. As Waterhay Lake became
shallower the reeds grew over the surface and dried up much of
the water. Now bushes and young trees are growing up, taking
up yet more water. This colonisation of marshland is an example
of what happens naturally, and shows why conservation has to
be an active process to keep habitats suitable for wildlife. Reed
cutting has cleared some parts and opened water channels, but
the bird hide overlooks dense reedbeds.

The car park at Waterhay is a good starting point for walks
around this corner of the Cotswold Water Park. There is a good
information board with directions for paths, or you can stay close
to the car park and gaze at the young Thames flowing under
Waterhay Bridge. Other activities include horse riding along the
bridleways nearby.

Did you know...
The Thames flows
from west to east –
a wildlife corridor
right across southern
Britain.

8 Cleveland Lakes

One of the best walks from Waterhay is to follow the Thames
Path towards Cricklade, until you see a signpost to Cleveland
Lakes. Take this short diversion from the path to two bird hides
by the lakes. The larger bird hide is a curious and creative design
built by the local community, and there is a small picnic area here
with good views of the lakes. The other birdwatching place is
about a quarter of a mile further to the north.

Orange-tip butterfly on the path beside Waterhay

Hide at Cleveland Lakes

Reeds spreading across Waterhay Lake

Elmlea Meadow

9 Elmlea Meadow

As you walk along the Thames Path between Cricklade and Waterhay, you will pass between two rectangular meadows [SU078450]. You may notice that the hedges are well kept, laid in a traditional fashion, with the stem of shrubs sliced to bend horizontally. With nearby copses, these meadows are ideal for wildlife. There are good notice boards explaining how the land is managed. The meadow is beside the circular walk described on page 36. It is close to National Cycle Network Route 45, which is the other way of getting to this reserve.

Borage in field margins provides nectar for insects

10 North Meadow

North Meadow is an important National Nature Reserve on the edge of Cricklade; it lies between the River Churn and the Thames. Although the Churn is counted as a tributary, it is longer from Cricklade to its source at Seven Springs than the Thames is from Cricklade to Thameshead. The Churn makes a significant increase to the water flowing into the main river.

North Meadow is a fine example of a flood meadow. Very wet in winter, it attracts wading birds, with the call of a curlew evoking that feeling of wilderness. In spring, there are large numbers of snake's head fritillaries, adder's tongue fern and marsh orchids. In summer, look for moths, damselflies and the meadow flowers (meadowsweet, lady's bedstraw, meadow rue) that last until the hay is cut in July. Reed buntings and sedge warblers can be heard along the River Churn and the Thames on either side of the meadow. Skylarks are present all year; for other birds, their singing may be territorial behaviour. For us it adds to the pleasure of walking here. There are several walks of a mile or two around the meadow and longer walks along the Thames Path. If you follow the Thames Path from North Meadow upstream, you will come to Elmlea Meadow (see page 34). If you go further, you will come to Cleveland Lakes.

The Thames becomes officially navigable at Cricklade Bridge. In the past, the river had enough water for cargo boats. Nowadays, the Thames between Cricklade and Lechlade is suitable only for canoes; and you may have to lift your craft over shallows and fallen trees. Canoeing is one of the best ways to explore waterways, because you move quietly and are looking forwards. You can get into the smaller streams (where passage is permitted) and feel very close to nature, with the reeds and the high banks hiding you and the wildlife from the rest of the world. Wonderful!

HOW TO GET THERE

North Meadow [SU100944]

Park the car in Cricklade and walk north to cross the Thames and enter North Meadow by a gate on the left-hand side of the road. Buses run to Cricklade from Cirencester and Swindon. It is also on National Cycle Network Route 45 from Cricklade.

www.naturalengland.org.uk/ourwork/conservation/designatedareas/nnr/1006112.aspx

Fritillaries at North Meadow

Waterhay car park ···· Cleveland Lakes ····
Elmlea ···· North Meadow ···· Cricklade ····
Waterhay Lake ···· Waterhay car park

8 MILES

This circular walk takes you to four of the nature reserves in the Cotswold Water Park. The path for the first part is smooth and hard, but becomes grassy and sometimes muddy near Elmlea and North Meadow.

Start at the car park at Waterhay Bridge. Take the bridleway going north and straight for nearly half a mile to a signpost and kissing gate on the right-hand side. Go through the gate, onto the path to Cleveland Lakes and Cricklade. This path takes you beside a large long lake that is sometimes used for rowing. Halfway along the lake is a shelter made from woven willows. At the eastern end of the lake, turn left and you come to a junction of the path to Cleveland Lakes bird hides and the Thames Path. The bird hides are worth the walk of half a mile before returning to this junction.

Follow the Thames Path signs pointing eastwards until you reach North Meadow. The Thames Path goes round three sides of Elmlea Meadow; it joins National Cycle Network Route 45, on the track bed of a former railway line, for a short distance before the bridge where the cycle path crosses the Thames (SU083947). Turn off the railway line to take the Thames Path beside the river and you will soon reach North Meadow. Here you can explore the meadow, looking for flowers and perhaps stop for a picnic. Halfway down the side of North Meadow, the Thames Path goes into a field used for horses. Take this route on the banks of the Thames until the Path crosses the river into a farm. The Thames Path turns right and doubles back to go into Cricklade. At the farm where the Thames Path doubles back, there is a short path to the entrance of the farmyard where there is a lane going south. Take this lane to Hallsfield, a road with houses on both sides. Turn right and take the second turning right, which should bring you to Cricklade Leisure Centre, Stones Lane SN6 6JW [SU093938]. The Leisure Centre (also signposted as Sports Centre) has a café and makes a good place to have a break halfway round the walk. You may

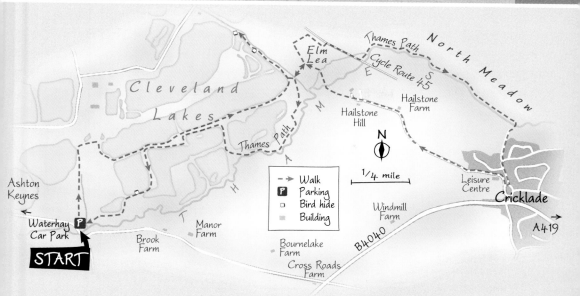

want to explore Cricklade, in which case you should find your own way to the Leisure Centre on the western edge of the town.

From Cricklade Leisure Centre, take the lane going northwest – not the cycle path that goes under the lane at an old railway bridge. The lane goes up a gentle hill to give you views over the meadows where you have been walking. It ends at Hailstone House. Go through the stone gateway and continue straight past the House along a bridleway that goes down to the Thames. Cross the narrow bridge, and keep on the path until you reach the Thames Path once more, signposted as a turning to the left. Take this left turn and you are walking back to the junction by Cleveland Lakes, where you were

nearly 4 miles earlier. Stay on the Thames Path to take a different route back to Waterhay.

The Thames Path to Waterhay goes through young woodland and is beside the river for some of the way, before looping round a large lake sometimes used for water skiing. When you are walking westwards, you may notice that the path you walked along in an easterly direction is on the other side of a ditch and a hedge. The Thames Path bends south and west again to go past the bird hide that overlooks the reeds in Waterhay Lake. From there it is a short distance back to the car park where you started.

Cleveland Lakes

11

Whelford Pools and Roundhouse Lake

⏵ HOW TO GET THERE

Whelford Pools [SU173995]

From Lechlade take the A417 towards Fairford. After about 2 miles, turn left onto the unclassified road for Whelford. Drive down this road for a mile. The entrance to the reserve is on the left with a small car park and cycle racks. The reserve is open to the public all year. The Thames Path is about 3 miles away. Whelford Pools can also be reached on an alternative route between Castle Eaton and Lechlade, which avoids walking along the A361. There is a track from High Street, Lechlade to Dudgrove Lane on the south side of Whelford Pools. This path passes the Roundhouse Lake Nature Reserve.

www.waterpark.org/leisure/whelford_pools.html

If you're not lucky enough to be able to canoe from Cricklade to Lechlade and have to walk instead, you will find that the Thames Path leaves the river at Inglesham, and travels beside the main road (A361). Hopefully, permission will at some point be given for a path that avoids this road, but in the meantime you could divert along minor roads and tracks and visit Whelford Pools – former gravel pits that were bought by the Gloucestershire Wildlife Trust in 1979. The two main lakes have become habitats for birds as the reeds have grown around the edges, and fallen trees have turned into handy perches (and a good habitat for insects). For birdwatchers, there are tufted duck, pochard, coot, mallard, great crested grebe, mute swans and herons. In winter, the pools are visited by widgeon and shoveler.

There are also three small pools favoured by dragonflies; the blue-bodied emperor, red-eyed damselfly and nine other species breed here. You will find two bird hides here, recently constructed by volunteers from Cirencester Rotary Club, and the good paths are suitable for people with limited mobility. There are posts with 'wind-up' recordings of bird songs placed around the reserve.

If you leave Whelford Pools to go along Dudgrove Lane on the south side of the Pools for a mile, you will find a track that goes to the High Street in Lechlade. A mile along this track is a reserve called Roundhouse Lake [SU198994], which is a lake with a bird hide. The name comes from the Round House at the junction of the Thames and Severn Canal and the River Thames, which is nearby.

12

Edward Richardson
and Phyllis Amey Reserve

Lechlade is the first Cotswold town you reach when travelling up the Thames; indeed it is the first town above Oxford, and as far up the Thames as most boats will go. It is well placed as a starting point to explore local nature reserves. There are meadows on the south side of the river (the side opposite the town) that are principally used as a recreational area. Lechlade provides the cafés and toilets that are not available at the reserves at Whelford, Cheese Wharf and the Edward Richardson and Phyllis Amey Reserve. This is on the northern edge of the town side of Lechlade, and is managed by the Gloucestershire Wildlife Trust. It is named after the man who first managed the reserve, and a member of the Amey family who helped with funds and equipment.

The shallow lakes are home to a rich variety of flora and fauna, in particular 15 species of dragonfly and damselfly. Along with bee orchids and southern marsh orchids, this reserve provides a home for a variety of wildlife throughout the year. The birds include the great crested grebe, sedge warblers, whitethroat and kingfishers. A visit in winter could well include sightings of fieldfare, brambling, widgeon, pochard and teal. There is a permitted path on the east and south of the lake.

 HOW TO GET THERE

Edward Richardson and Phyllis Amey Reserve [SP 215008]

The reserve is off the A316, north of Lechlade. At the first roundabout, travelling from Lechlade, take the first exit into a cul-de-sac opposite Horseshore Lake. You can park in the cul-de-sac. The Thames Path and boat moorings are 1½ miles away in Lechlade.

www.wildlifetrusts.org/
reserves/edward-richardson-
and-phyllis-amey

The larger lake at Edward Richardson and Phyllis Amey Reserve

13 Cheese Wharf

Moving downstream from Lechlade, the first reserve is a small but fascinating National Trust property called Cheese Wharf. It is part of the National Trust's Buscot and Coleshill Estate, but is not mentioned much in the guides to this area. It is, as its name suggests, the remains of a wharf where you can park and picnic. It lies between the main road (the A417), and a bend in the river upstream from Buscot. Cheese Wharf is now little more than a peaceful place to park and watch the river and its wildlife. Imagine it as it used to be – bustling with carts loaded with cheeses and other farm produce to be taken by boat to Oxford and London. While this book emphasises walking, cycling and boating, don't overlook the opportunity for watching wildlife while sitting in a car (preferably when the car is stationary!). For bird photography, a car becomes a hide, and the window ledge a camera rest.

The Thames at Cheese Wharf

14 Buscot Weir

Buscot is a pretty village, with a car park, tea shop and toilets. The wildlife interest is down by the river and the meadow by the weir pool. Walk from the village down to the lock and you will see, on your right, the meadow by the weir pool – an ideal picnic spot. Crossing the weir to the lock, you pass a beautiful small cottage which the National Trust lets for holidays. On the far side of the lock, there are excellent information boards telling the history of the area.

If you want to continue walking, there is a good circular route of about 3 miles using the Thames Path from Buscot Lock to a footbridge at what is called Eaton Weir (not actually a weir, but there used to be a flash lock here). Cross the footbridge, passing a small cottage and boat moorings to a footpath going southwest towards the A417. At the A417, go north along a track and you will find a footpath back to the meadow by Buscot Weir. The main National Trust property is Buscot House and Park, which has an entrance from the main road about a mile from Buscot going towards Faringdon.

 HOW TO GET THERE

Buscot Weir [SU231978] and Cheese Wharf [SU224983]

Buscot lies on the A417 between Faringdon and Lechlade. From the main road, take the lane between the cottages towards the river until you reach the National Trust car park [SU231977]. From there, walk to Buscot Lock and Weir, with a meadow beside the weir pool. Cheese Wharf is on the A417, about half a mile from Buscot [SU224984]. The Thames Path goes by Buscot Weir, on the opposite side of the river to Cheese Wharf.

Buscot House and Park: www. buscot-park.com/visitor-info

Buscot Weir pool

Did you know...
The Thames is 215 miles in length from source to sea and is the longest English river.

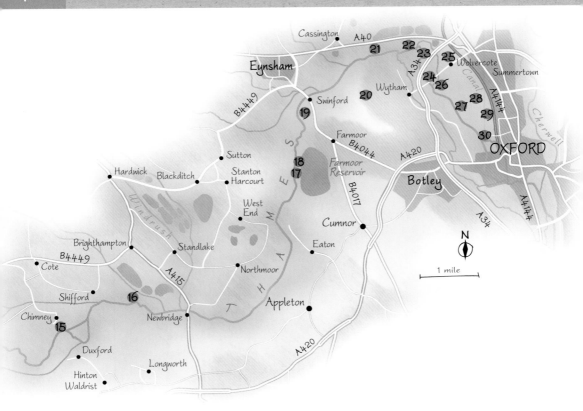

3. West Oxfordshire to North Oxford

From Lechlade to Oxford, the Thames runs through open
country, and there are no riverside towns or villages for more
than 30 miles. Consequently, access by public transport is very
limited, and the paths are sometimes wet and muddy – so
walking and boating are the best ways to explore this area.
Only boats less than 7½ feet high can pass beneath Osney
Bridge in Oxford. The Thames Path is not a designated cycle
track in this section, although people manage to cycle on parts
of it. Generally this is a quiet part of the river, and it is rich in
wildlife. If the electricity pylons striding across this landscape
are an eyesore, then be comforted by the thought that the rest
is beautiful all year round.

*Boardwalk to the bird hides
at Chimney Meadows*

Picnic area near the Thames Path at Chimney Meadows

15 Chimney Meadows

 HOW TO GET THERE

Chimney Meadows [SP360010]

Chimney is a small hamlet, near Bampton, West Oxon OX18 2EH. It is reached by minor roads from Tadpole Bridge or the village of Aston. There is no easy way to get to Chimney Meadows by public transport. The Thames Path runs between the river and the reserve, with an entrance close to where the Thames Path crosses Shifford Lock Cut. You can moor at Newbridge and Tadpole Bridge.

www.bbowt.org.uk

Chimney Meadows are full of flowers in spring and summer, and are good nesting grounds for curlews and skylarks. If you are lucky you may see an otter in the river, or roe deer on the meadows. The old concrete pill-boxes are used by bats.

For people walking along the Thames Path between Tadpole Bridge and Newbridge, the picnic tables near the entrance by Shifford Lock Cut make this an attractive place to stop. There are good walks around the reserve and to the pubs at Newbridge and Tadpole Bridge. A circular walk by the Thames Path and the Windrush Way is described on pages 46-47. There is good wheelchair access to the bird hides. Volunteers are welcomed by the Berks, Bucks & Oxon Wildlife Trust (BBOWT).

16

Standlake Common

Standlake Common used to be farmland before the gravel was extracted. Since 2000, Oxfordshire County Council, the mineral company and the landowner have worked together to make wetland habitats suitable for wildlife, creating a new nature reserve next to the River Thames. The lake has gravel beaches, and shallows where aquatic plants grow, providing homes for invertebrate animals. These attract ducks and wading birds, thus enriching the variety of wildlife in this area.

The grassland is managed as a traditional hay meadow, grazed by sheep after the hay is cut in late summer. The boundary hedgerows, the willow and hawthorn scrub provide cover for small birds and mammals. The public access is restricted to the bird hides, which are usually locked. Keys can be bought from the Lower Windrush Valley Project manager (tel: 01865 815 426). For most visitors, the reserve has to be viewed through gaps in the hedges or from the River Thames, which runs on the southern side of the reserve.

The Windrush Way has interesting mosaic sculptures and there is a picnic area with information by the reserve. There are riverside pubs at Newbridge.

HOW TO GET THERE

Standlake Common [SP398015]

Standlake, West Oxon. It is reached by the Windrush Way (Newbridge to Witney). The Thames Path is accessible at Newbridge where there are moorings. The reserve is about a mile from Newbridge along the Windrush Way.

www.oxfordshire.gov.uk/cms/content/standlake-common-nature-reserve (email to apply for key to bird hide: lwvp@oxfordshire.gov.uk)

Mosaic sculpture near Standlake Common

Standlake Common

Chimney Meadows Reserve ···· Standlake Common ···· Newbridge ···· Chimney Meadows Reserve

8 MILES

This walk is best in late spring and summer when the meadows are in full bloom. It crosses a ford that is usually 2 inches deep in summer, but may be much deeper in winter. There is rough ground and some very muddy patches, so boots are advised.

It is recommended that you go around this circular walk as directed (in a clockwise direction), so that you come to the ford early on in the walk. If it looks too deep for you to cross, you will not have far to retrace your steps.

Starting at Chimney Meadows Reserve car park [SP353012], walk east beside the metalled track and continue straight on, along a grass path across meadows, following the line of

Ford across the Great Brook

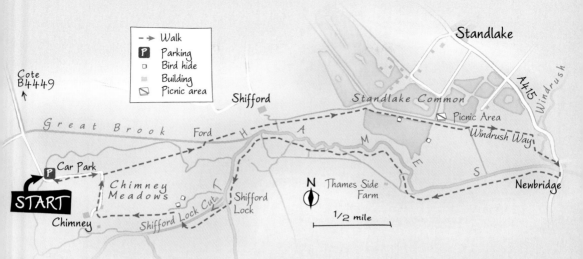

the pylons. Divert to the bird hides where signposted if you wish, or visit them when you come back.

After leaving Chimney Meadows, you will find yourself walking beside the Great Brook until you come to a ford. On the far side of the ford, go through the kissing gates, and walk diagonally across the meadow, passing under the pylons to reach a muddy area between two gateways. The footpath is poorly marked in this area. Keeping parallel to the line of pylons, but slightly to the north of them, walk along the edge of two more fields until you reach a path that runs between two lakes. The lake on your right (southern) side is Standlake Common. After a sign that tells you this, take a path on the right that is the Windrush Way. This goes down beside Standlake Common and passes a bird hide on your right. At the end of the lake is a 'crossroads' of paths. Langdon Lane on your right goes to another bird hide. You should go straight on at this 'crossroads', passing a picnic area on your left [SP392019]. This is worth a

visit to get more information about the Lower Windrush Project and the mosaics along the way. Where the footpath meets the A415 road, take a path through a kissing gate to wind your way to cross the River Windrush close to a pill-box. Soon you will find yourself at Newbridge, with a choice of pubs on either side of the Thames.

From Newbridge, the route back to Chimney Meadows Reserve is easy, along the well-marked Thames Path. In summer listen for warblers in the reeds on the riverbank. At other times of year, you can expect to hear and see curlews. The Thames Path crosses over an arched footbridge onto a large island planted with poplar trees. This is part of Chimney Reserve, as shown by the number of nesting boxes. The Thames Path goes over Shifford Lock Cut on a wooden bridge. Cross the bridge, go along the broad track straight ahead into the reserve, passing a picnic area on your left. The track becomes a metalled road that leads back to the car park.

17 Shrike Meadow

Shrike Meadow from
Farmoor Reservoir

The nature reserves at Farmoor Reservoir are a fine example of how water companies can use their resources to protect wildlife and re-create wilderness areas with public access. Shrike Meadow was a grassy meadow, named because a great grey shrike was seen there in the winter of 1998–9. In the year 2000, it became a reserve when a long lagoon and shallow ponds were excavated and 3,500 reeds were planted. It lies between Farmoor Reservoir and the Thames and is about 10 acres in size. When river levels are high, water can flow into the lagoon, allowing small fish to move in and out.

There is a bird hide at the southern end of the reserve, which is reached by a path from the riverbank. There is another hide on the reservoir wall which overlooks the lagoon and has a magnificent view of the West Oxfordshire countryside. This hide at the reservoir is accessible in a wheelchair, with a parking place close by. The hides are usually unlocked in the day; if not, a key is available at the reservoir office. Farmoor Reservoir is very popular with birdwatchers; you will often be able to get advice from the staff or other visitors.

There is fishing available on the reservoir, which is also used for sailing. There is also an interesting walk around the reservoir along footpaths below the reservoir wall. This will take you past another small reserve called Buckthorn Meadow, which is a dense reedbed with bushes at the margins. This is fenced off and has no access, but you may see and hear warblers and reed buntings on the edges. In the spring of 2012, another long pond was created here.

Did you know...
There are 18 river catchments flowing into the main River Thames.

18

Pinkhill Meadow

Pinkhill Meadow was created as a reserve in a space between the reservoir and a loop in the river. It was opened in 1992 and, like Shrike Meadow, has an area of 10 acres. In addition to the grassland, there is a small lake, many small ponds, reeds and scrub between the river and Farmoor Reservoir. The bird hide is beside the lake and has the best views of birds in this cluster of reserves, including an island used by nesting birds. There is a disabled parking space close to the bird hide.

The path beside the river gives views through the reeds and a chance to see dragonflies. This route was the old towpath from Pinkhill Lock to the ferry at Bablockhythe. Unfortunately there was not a ferry service at the time of writing.

Looking east from Farmoor, you will see Wytham Wood, another recommended reserve.

Pinkhill Meadow lake

 HOW TO GET THERE

Shrike Meadow [SP438062] and Pinkhill Meadow [SP440068]

Farmoor Reservoir, west of Oxford. There is a car park at Farmoor Reservoir (Gate 3), with disabled parking close to the bird hides. From the Thames Path at Pinkhill Lock, look for a path going upstream beside the river on the Farmoor (east) side. Pinkhill Meadow is a quarter of a mile from the lock. Shrike Meadow is half a mile further on. There is good mooring above Pinkhill Lock. The S2 bus service from Oxford to Witney passes through Farmoor.

www.thameswater.co.uk

19 Swinford Meadows

The Swinford meadows are typical flood meadows, with natural muddy ditches, coarse grasses and marshy areas filled with sedges. You will find them when walking along the Thames Path between Pinkhill and Eynsham Locks [SP442083]. The meandering route of the river is very noticeable here – most people cut across some of the loops to shorten the path. Once a river is running round a bend, it tends to erode the outer side of the bend more than the inner side, so the bend becomes deeper. The more the river bends, the more the erosion occurs, until the bend is so great that the river cuts across the bend to create an island. From the Thames Path, look across the river to see an example of this – there is an island with a shallow reed-filled

Swinford Bridge near Eynsham

channel on the far side.

Swinford meadows can only be reached by the Thames Path, but there is a circular walk by footpaths from Eynsham to Pinkhill Lock, the Thames Path to Eynsham Lock, and from Eynsham Lock back to the village by footpaths and roadside paths.

Swinford is the name of the small group of houses, farm and water-treatment works around Eynsham Lock, and the name derives from the ford that was once the way of crossing the river – which was normally shallow enough for pigs (swine) to cross. The story is that John Wesley nearly drowned here in 1764, and a bridge was built in 1769 to prevent such accidents. It is a toll bridge, but walking and cycling across are free (rightly so!).

20 Wytham Wood

▶ HOW TO GET THERE

Wytham Wood [SP468085]

Keeper's Hill, Wytham OX2
8QQ, to the northwest of
Oxford. A car park is at the
top of the road leading from
Wytham village. There are
two other entrances from
Botley (some parking) and
from Swinford (no parking).
A permit is required from the
University of Oxford. Cycling
is not allowed in the woods,
but Wytham is a pleasant
cycle ride along the lanes
from Wolvercote. If coming by
boat, moor at Eynsham Lock,
and walk to the Swinford
gate. Open from 10am to
dusk.

http://herbaria.plants.ox.ac.
uk/wytham/index.php

Wytham Wood was given to the University of Oxford in 1942
by the ffennel family after the death of their daughter, Hazel.
There is a memorial stone marking this gift beside the Singing
Way in the Wood. The University uses the 960 acres of woodland
for ecology studies. There are some plantations of conifers, but
most of the wood is old semi-natural woodland – the bluebells
are beautiful in spring. The habitats vary from ancient trees to
plantations, and from ponds to grassland. The rich fauna and
flora are well documented with more than 800 species of moths
and butterflies.

The Singing Way has lovely views of Oxford and the upper
Thames Valley, and it is said that the name was given to this
area because pilgrims would burst into song when they saw the
spires of Oxford. There are many miles of paths to explore, but
the most popular is a circular walk up the grassy slope from the
Keeper's Hill car park, turning right along Singing Way – a broad
gravel track – and right where it meets another broad gravel
track, which winds its way through the trees and back to the car
park. This route is suitable for pushchairs, but would be difficult
for wheelchairs because of several steep sections and the kissing
gates. There are seats at the best viewpoints, but no toilets or
other facilities in the woods.

There are information boards with maps at the car parks at
Keeper's Hill and Botley entrances. Dogs are not allowed. Guided
visits can be arranged. The woods are closed for one or two
weeks each year for deer culling. The White Hart pub in Wytham
village is the closest for refreshments.

*Primroses in
Wytham Wood*

21 Yarnton Mead &
22 Oxey Mead

Yarnton Mead and Oxey Mead are two adjacent flood meadows
that have been grazed since medieval times. They lie between
the Thames and the main A40 road, a short distance west of
Oxford. Yarnton Mead is managed by 'fai farms', and Oxey Mead
belongs to the Berks, Bucks & Oxon Wildlife Trust (BBOWT).

Spring and summer flowers are abundant, including marsh
orchids. There are many butterflies in summer. There are usually
skylarks, reed buntings by the river, and occasionally curlew.
Often you'll find yourself the only visitor, though the traffic
noise on the A40 may be a bit intrusive. Dogs are permitted if
there are no grazing animals, but they must be kept on the lead.
The meads are open at all times.

Apart from one information board, there are no facilities at
these meadows. On the north (opposite) side of the A40, there
are several lakes (no access, but visible from the cycle path) with
plenty of water birds, including terns and gulls nesting in spring.
The terns can be admired as they hunt for fish in the Thames.

HOW TO GET THERE

Yarnton Mead and Oxey Mead [SP478107]

Between the Thames and the
main A40 road, northwest
of Oxford. Oxey Mead and
Yarnton Mead are next to
each other. There is a gateway
on the A40 with a BBOWT
sign, and there is room to
park a car on the grass verge
(please don't block the cycle
track/footpath or gateway).
The Thames Path is on the
opposite side of the river,
and is not accessible. A path
beside the Duke's Cut leads
through to the Oxford Canal
and its towpath (the best
way to reach this site on
foot). There is a cycle path by
the A40, Oxford to Witney.
Mooring is possible at the
upstream end of Yarnton
Mead, and the riverbank
at the entrance to Duke's
Cut is a place often used
for overnight and daytime
mooring.

www.bbowt.org.uk
www.faifarms.co.uk

Oxey Mead in spring

Visitor centre
at Kings Lock

HOW TO GET THERE

**Kings Lock and Pixey Mead
[SP481103]**

This reserve and visitor centre at Kings Lock can only be reached on foot or by boat. There is open access to Pixey Mead by a footpath across the weir by Kings Lock. The nearest public car park is in Godstow Road, Wolvercote. Patrons of the Trout Inn, by Godstow Bridge, can use that car park. The Thames Path runs by Kings Lock, and here is a good place to sit for a rest along the way. Boats can moor overnight or to picnic on the banks of Pixey Mead.

23 Pixey Mead

Pixey Mead is a flood meadow with masses of cowslips in spring. It is isolated, being bounded by the Thames, Duke's Cut, Wolvercote Stream and the A34 dual carriageway.

This place makes a good walk before or after lunch at the Trout Inn. Unfortunately, the traffic noise on the A34 intrudes on the peace, but you can still enjoy the song of the larks.

An attractive visitor centre at Kings Lock gives information about the plants, birds and insects. The centre has an interesting construction, being made from straw bales and wood. There is a campsite at the lock that is run by the Environment Agency.

24 Wolvercote Orchard

If you are at the Trout Inn, look at Wolvercote Community Orchard which is between the Trout Inn car park and the allotments [SP485094]. This is a traditional orchard with a wide variety of apple trees. Managed without potent insecticides, the grass and trees are home to insects that naturally control the pests. It is open for people to walk round and see the fruit growing, and it is an easy walk from the Godstow Road public car park. To taste the different varieties, 'apple days' are held in the autumn.

Wolvercote Orchard

25 Wolvercote Lakes

Two lakes beside the railway in Wolvercote are owned by the Oxford Preservation Trust, and are being turned into a nature conservation site. The lakes were originally known as 'pleasure lakes', created when the railway was built above the floodplain of Port Meadow. There was once a small house on stilts beside the lakes, but no trace exists today.

In 2012, work was started to create shallow areas around the lakes, and to build pond-dipping platforms and a bird hide. Local volunteers have started to clear non-native plants, and to sow native hazel, hawthorn, and wild roses for hedges. These will provide food and shelter for birds and small mammals.

One of the lakes can be viewed from the roadside [SP493097], but the reserve is usually shut. Information about open days should be sought at the Oxford Preservation Trust (www.oxfordpreservation.org.uk/land/wolvercotelakes. php; tel: 01865 242 918).

A corner of the Wolvercote Lakes

26 Wolvercote Common &

27 Port Meadow

Port Meadow and Wolvercote Common are a single large expanse of floodplain. Wolvercote Common, the northern part, belongs to the villagers of Wolvercote, who still have grazing rights. Port Meadow, the southern part, was granted as common land to the citizens of Oxford by Alfred the Great. It has remained as uncultivated pasture land beside the Thames. Lying close to north Oxford, and only a mile away from the city centre, it has always been a popular place for open air activity. In the 19th century, it was used for military displays and for horse races. During the First World War, there was a small airfield at the northern end. A small burial mound, called the Round Hill, shows that it was occupied in the Bronze Age. A raised causeway across Port Meadow to Medley was one of the routes from Oxford to the west, crossing the Thames by fords at the top end of Fiddler's Island. The southern end of Port Meadow was used as a rubbish dump by Victorians living in north Oxford.

Port Meadow and Wolvercote Common have a spacious open feeling, and are at their most beautiful in a morning mist or an evening sunset. The middle area becomes flooded every autumn and remains wet until June. Widgeon, teal and a few shovellers over-winter on this flooded area. Waders appear during their migrations and some over-winter; a few redshank and the occasional oyster-catcher remain in summer. Black-headed gulls, mallard, greylag geese and mute swans are present all year

Port Meadow in June

A dragonfly laying eggs

round. Herons and an occasional little egret hunt in the flooded area, or along the riverbank when the meadow is dry. There is a good circular walk along the Thames Path on the west bank of the river and back across Port Meadow (if not too flooded). This could include a visit to the famous Trout Inn (now a restaurant).

For much of the year, larks can be heard singing above Wolvercote Common. In summer, reed warblers skulk and sing in the willow and shrubs at the edges.

In the river itself, coots can be seen nesting among the moored boats at Medley. They, together with great crested grebes and cormorants, are present all year. Kingfishers are rarely seen here, because there are no suitable nesting sites and few fishing perches.

The meadow is so large that it never feels crowded, and is popular for picnics in summer. Some people swim in the Thames from the banks, which have small gravel beaches when the water-level is low. The flooded area can become frozen enough for skating in mid-winter. Rowing boats can be hired from the landing stage for the Perch Inn. Fishing is popular.

For Wolvercote Common, there is a good car park with toilets in Godstow Road at the top (northern) end.

For food and drink, the choice is wide – from the Trout Inn and Red Lion pub in Wolvercote, the Perch Inn at Binsey, to cafés and pubs in Jericho.

 HOW TO GET THERE

Port Meadow and Wolvercote Common [SP502073]

Port Meadow is reached by Walton Well Street and Aristotle Lane in Jericho, Oxford, and by the Thames Path at the southwest corner. Wolvercote Meadow has two entrances in Godstow Road, Wolvercote. There is temporary mooring for small boats and canoes. Overnight mooring is possible above Godstow Lock or, with permission, at Bossom's Boatyard. The area is easy to reach and cross by cycling. There is car parking at Godstow Road (north end) and Walton Well Street (southeast corner). There are bus services to Wolvercote (number 9) and Jericho (number 17). There is a railway station 1 mile away, reached via the Thames Path or the canal path. If pushing a wheelchair or pushchair, you will find the route is flat, but paths are rough and limited. The gateways are a bit narrow and can be muddy in winter. There are no restrictions for dogs.

www. visitoxfordandoxfordshire. com/see-and-do/Parks-and-gardens.aspx

28 Burgess Field

HOW TO GET THERE

Burgess Field [SP499080]

In Port Meadow, look for a hard track of worn concrete going north from the Walton Well Street entrance – Burgess Field is at the end of this track. There are also two kissing gates on the north side of Burgess Field, which link to Wolvercote Common, where the ground may be wet and muddy.

www.
visitoxfordandoxfordshire.
com/see-and-do/Parks-
andgardens.aspx

Burgess Field was a city council landfill site until the 1970s, but was converted to woodland and meadow. Nowadays, the council deposit the subsoil dug from graves in Oxford Cemetery across the meadow land to fill in dips with a soil poor in nutrients, thus encouraging wildflowers. Roe and muntjac deer are sometimes seen. Burgess Field is not grazed by cattle or horses, so offers cowpat-free picnics. The path around the circumference is a popular morning run for joggers.

Meadow flowers in Burgess Field

29 Trap Grounds Town Green

The Trap Grounds in Oxford are a great example of local community conservation. This was a rubbish dump, then an area designated for building, but unused. It is conserved by local volunteers after a ruling in the House of Lords determined that this was common land used by local people. There is a small lake, reedbed, woodland and a small meadow. In January 2012, snipe, water rail, reed bunting, bullfinch and greater spotted woodpecker were all recorded here.

Workdays are arranged by the Friends of the Trap Grounds and Oxfordshire Conservation Volunteers – all are welcome. Children at the primary school on one side of the reserve have helped with tree planting, and use the reserve and the nearby Port Meadow for an After-school Environment Club.

The Anchor pub in Hayfield Road is popular for meals.

 HOW TO GET THERE

Trap Grounds Town Green [SP504082]

The reserve is entered from the Oxford canal towpath by Frenchay Road Bridge, north Oxford. It is within walking distance from the centre of Oxford and the station via the Oxford canal. It is also a short walk from Port Meadow, along Aristotle Lane and the canal path. Bus services along the Woodstock Road are the closest (stop near Frenchay Road). Parking in nearby streets is possible. It is on National Cycle Network Route 51 on the canal towpath. The Thames Path is about a mile away, across Port Meadow.

www.trap-grounds.org.uk

30 Fiddler's Island

Fiddler's Island in Oxford [SP50072] is a long narrow area between the main channel of the Thames and a side-stream that becomes little more than a ditch between the island and the allotments at Cripley Meadow. It is managed more by neglect than active conservation, but it is a wilderness to explore. In summer there are flowers on the riverbank beside the Thames Path which runs the length of the island. There is access across Rainbow Bridge beside Bossom's Boatyard at Medley, from Port Meadow, and by a bridge over the Sheepwash Channel near the railway station.

The way into Trap Grounds Town Green

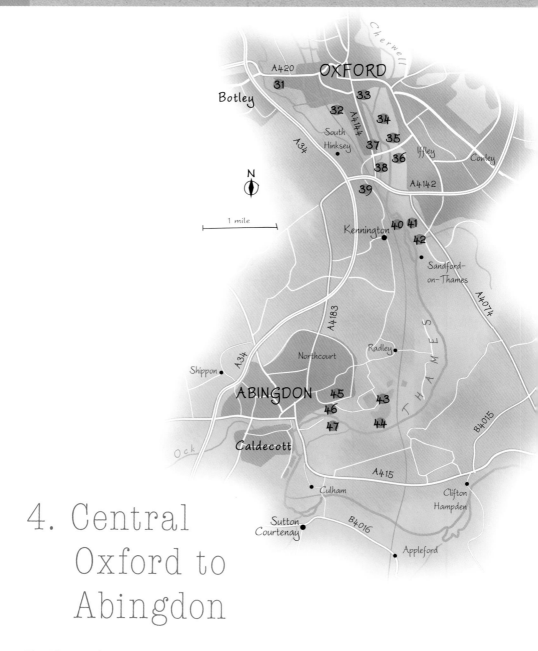

4. Central Oxford to Abingdon

The Thames from central Oxford to Abingdon has more nature reserves per mile of river than any other area. This is due to local efforts in conserving land that has always been flood meadow and in restoring land that was used for other purposes. This part of the river is full of local history, beginning and ending at two ancient abbeys, Osney and Abingdon.

The Thames by Christchurch Meadow

Flowers on North
Hinksey Meadow

31 North Hinksey Meadow

HOW TO GET THERE

**North Hinksey Meadow
[SP497058]**

North Hinksey Meadow lies
between Hinksey and Osney
in Oxford. From the Botley
Road in Oxford, go down
to the end of Ferry Hinksey
Lane, and take the path that
leads towards Hinksey. The
meadow is about a quarter of
a mile along the track on the
north (right) side. There are
two kissing gate entrances.
The track is National Cycle
Network Route 57 to Hinksey
and Cumnor.

www.oxfordpreservation.
org.uk/land/hinksey.php

North Hinksey Meadow has always been a flood meadow
managed for haymaking and grazing. There are many
wildflowers in spring, including fritillaries. At the top end of the
meadow there is a path through the Seacourt Nature Park to the
Botley Road. If you walk into North Hinksey, and turn left along
North Hinksey Lane, you will reach the Fishes, a riverside pub
that serves good meals.

The stream on the west side of North Meadow is the
Seacourt Stream which runs from the Thames above Kings Lock,
through Wytham. Below North Hinksey Meadow, the Seacourt
Stream divides into the Bulstake Stream which goes back to the
Thames at Osney, and the Hinksey Stream which runs down to
Kennington. These backwaters can be explored by canoe, which
is a lovely way to get a really close view of the wildlife.

32 Grandpont Nature Reserve

Walking along the Thames Path between Folly Bridge and Osney, you will come to Grandpont Nature Reserve [SP508055], which is a green space recovered from part of the former Oxford gas works. The nature reserve has small meadows between copses and a few marshy patches. The plant and animal wildlife are all common species, which can be charming when the bluebells are in flower under the trees, and blackbirds sing while blue tits dart among the bushes. The spaciousness of Grandpont is enhanced by the adjacent playing field and the meadows on the other side of the railway line.

The gas holders were demolished in 1968, and the only remaining structure is the former railway bridge across the river. From this bridge, now used as a footpath and cycle path, you can reach the point where the Castle Mill Stream enters the Thames. There is a pleasant walk beside this stream that brings you to Oxford Castle. From there, it is easy to complete a circle via Carfax at the centre of Oxford and St Aldates to get back to the river at Folly Bridge.

> Did you know...
> The Thames flows through eight counties, London, and 16 other cities and major towns.

Grandpont Nature Reserve

Christ Church Meadow

33 Christ Church Meadow

HOW TO GET THERE

Christ Church Meadow (SP516058)

Christ Church Meadow is an ancient green space in the centre of Oxford. There are two entrances in St Aldates, one through the Memorial Garden, and another behind the Head of the River pub. There is a gate between Merton College and Corpus Christi in Merton Lane, and a gate at the eastern end of the meadow next to the Botanic Gardens. The gates are open from early morning to dusk every day. From the Thames Path, cross Folly Bridge to find the entrances in St Aldates. It is within easy walking distance of the centre of Oxford. Buses from the Redbridge Park and Ride go to St Aldates.

www.chch.ox.ac.uk/visiting/meadow

Christ Church Meadow is good for picnics, for watching the river, and for views of the various Oxford colleges. The meadow was once threatened by plans to build an inner ring road in Oxford. However, the traffic flow in Oxford is sluggish at best, and another stretch of concrete would have made no difference. So visit this meadow and rejoice in the resistance to more roads in the wrong places. The wild part of the meadow is grazed by cattle and is fenced off from the paths. The paths are firm and suitable for wheelchairs, but the entrance through the Memorial Gardens is the only one that it is possible to enter with a wheelchair. The other gates are kissing gates, designed in times when people were smaller. Visitors are asked to note the rules about access to, and use of, the meadow that are posted at the meadow entrances.

From Christ Church Meadow, you can watch rowing and punting on the Thames and the Cherwell, and walk onto an island in the mouth of the Cherwell in front of the college boathouses.

Aston's Eyot

▶ HOW TO GET THERE

Aston's Eyot [SP523052]
The Kidneys [SP525048]
Meadow Lane Nature Park
[SP527043]

There are entrances in Jackdaw Lane and Meadow Lane, east Oxford. These are three reserves on the east side of the Thames between the mouth of the Cherwell and Iffley Lock. Aston's Eyot is the first (going north to south) and has entrances at the bottom end of Jackdaw Lane and in the Kidneys. The Kidneys is next to Aston's Eyot, and is entered directly from Meadow Lane. Meadow Lane is a small area to the south of Donnington Bridge Road, between Salter's boatyard and the Boundary Brook. There is no official mooring on this side of the river, but small boats can tie up for picnics and to watch regattas. The Thames Path is on the opposite side of the river. There are no public car parks nearby, but street parking is possible. Buses run from the centre of Oxford along the Iffley Road.

www.friendsofastonseyot.org.uk

www.visitoxfordand oxfordshire.com/see-and-do/Parks-and-gardens.aspx/

34 Aston's Eyot

Aston's Eyot is actively conserved by a group of volunteers who have built bird boxes and cut back scrub. It is an island that is mostly wooded, but there are clear spaces by the river. It was once a rubbish tip, but is now inhabited by roe and muntjac deer, rabbits, bats, moles and shrews; and a variety of common butterflies enjoy the brambles and nettles in summer.

35 The Kidneys

The Kidneys [SP525048] has a central meadow surrounded by scrub, trees and ditches – ideal for adventurous children and picnics. Mooring is possible for small boats during the day.

All three sites on Meadow Lane have the classic Thames-side pollarded willows. Pollarding is essential to stop the trees cracking open, and the branches falling across the river. As the tree trunks get older and thicker, they become better homes for insects and birds.

36 Meadow Lane Nature Park

Meadow Lane Nature Park [SP527043] is small and there is less to explore. It is between Salter's boatyard and a stream, Boundary Brook, running through an open concrete channel. This stream has arisen in Headington, where the Lea Valley is a Local Nature Reserve, and has wound its way through Cowley to reach the Thames. Brambles are the major vegetation, so the park is well worth a visit in the blackberry season (usually September). Remember, brambles are a good source of food for insects, and provide shelter for small mammals.

Meadow Lane Nature Park viewed from Iffley Meadows

37 Long Bridges Nature Park

 HOW TO GET THERE

Long Bridges Nature Park [SP524046]

Donnington Bridge Road, Oxford OX4 4AX. Enter from the Thames Path which runs between the reserve and the main channel of the Thames. The nearest official car park is at the Redbridge Park and Ride, in the Abingdon Road, about half a mile away. Buses from central Oxford run along the Abingdon Road. Cycling is permitted along this part of the Thames Path. There is a mooring place close to Long Bridges, and more spaces near Iffley Lock and upstream.

www.oxford.gov.uk/ PageRender/decLP/Nature_ Reserves_occw.htm

This park is beside a former bathing pool in one of the side-streams of the Thames running through Oxford. It is a good place for a picnic and to watch events on the river, and was cleared and improved in the autumn of 2011. Its features are willows, blackberries and grassy glades. Canoeists can explore the side-stream down to the weirs, and enter a network of backwaters. Iffley Meadows are on the other side of Weirs Lane.

Willow in flower, Long Bridges

Fritillaries in Iffley Meadows

38 Iffley Meadows

These are ancient flood meadows, with lots of fritillaries in spring, which are counted by volunteers (Berks, Bucks & Oxon Wildlife Trust (BBOWT)). In the marshier area on the south southern side, there are lots of cuckoo-flowers that appear at about the same time as the fritillaries. There are walks through and around the meadows to streams and corners of scrubland. Resident birds include meadow pipits, water rail and snipe. Iffley Lock nearby has the remains of an early pound lock, now functioning as one of the weirs. Iffley village has a pretty Norman church and several pubs.

Iffley Church

Christic Church Meadow ···· Meadow Lane ···· Folly Bridge ···· Christ Church Meadow

5¼ MILES

Starting at Folly Bridge, go down the side of the Head of the River pub and find a tall kissing gate into Christ Church Meadow. The gate is narrow and awkward if you are carrying a large rucksack or pushing a buggy. Walk beside the river and follow the path that curves left along the bank of the Cherwell until you pass the Botanic Gardens and find another tall narrow kissing gate that brings you into Rose Lane. Go up the lane and turn right to walk over Magdalen Bridge. Walk from the roundabout (called The Plain) along Iffley Road until you find Jackdaw Lane. Note the sportsground where Roger Bannister ran the first 4 minute mile.

Turn right into Jackdaw Lane and go to the end where you will enter Aston's Eyot. There is a network of paths around the Eyot, which you can explore until you find the other entrance on the southeast side where you cross a stream to the Kidneys Nature Reserve.

If you cross the meadow in the middle of the Kidneys, you will find a path to Meadow Lane. Walk along Meadow Lane until you reach Donnington Bridge Road. Cross the road to continue along Meadow Lane behind the City of Oxford Rowing Club and Salter's boatyard. Immediately after Salter's is the entrance to Meadow Lane Nature Reserve.

Continue along Meadow Lane until you reach Church Way in Iffley. If you have time, it is well worth visiting Iffley Church, which has Norman archways and a history to match. From Church Way, take Mill Lane to a narrow road that is signposted to Iffley Lock.

Cross the lock, and walk back towards Oxford along the riverside path, past the Isis Farmhouse (a pub with a riverside garden) and a boathouse, and you will find a gateway into Iffley Meadows. Take the path crossing diagonally across the first meadow and continue along the footpath, which leaves the meadows by a kissing gate to a path across

Iffley Meadow

the weirs before emerging at the point where Donnington Bridge Road becomes Weir Lane. Cross the road and turn right to walk towards the bridge, and you will find a gateway into Long Bridges. This is opposite another gate, usually locked, into Iffley Meadows.

Wander through Long Bridges Nature Park, either directly to the bank of the Thames or past the former bathing place where there is still a picnic area. Continue up the towpath past boathouses, meadows and playing fields, and you will reach Folly Bridge where you started.

Alternatives to this walk are: 1) hire a boat or punt at Folly Bridge and visit these reserves by water; 2) shorten the walk by crossing the river at Donnington Bridge, which misses going through Iffley (about 1½ miles shorter); and 3) extend the walk by going half a mile upstream from Folly Bridge on the Thames Path (west) side to visit Grandpont, coming back over the former gas works bridge and along the other (east) side to St Aldates or Folly Bridge.

39 Kennington Pools

Kennington Pools is a little-known reserve, hidden between Oxford's southern ring road and the railway line; it was created as a pit when earth was used to build the railway in the 19th century. It has a variety of habitats that are surrounded by a rare example of UK wet woodland habitat. The raised banks between the pools increase the marginal aquatic areas for wetland plants like water dock, greater pond sedge and common valerian. A diversity of invertebrate species, including molluscs, a nationally scarce water beetle and eight species of dragonfly, have been recorded in the pools.

The trees in the reserve include ash, crack willows, silver birch, hazel, grey willow, goat willow, alder, sycamore and horse chestnut. As a result of the damp conditions, these trees can support a range of mosses and liverworts. Shrubs (guelder rose, elder, hawthorn, buckthorn, blackthorn and wild current) provide food and shelter for many species at the site. The woodland floor sustains bluebells, enchanter's nightshade, dog's mercury, giant fescue and remote sedge. Black bryony and hop can be found climbing some of the shrubs and trees.

The plans for conservation management of this reserve are an example of what is, or could be, done on other reserves. One aim is to improve the wet areas, by selective clearing of some trees. Reducing the tree canopy makes a mixture of open and shaded habitats. The open areas allow lower plants to grow, with more shelter and food for animals, while removing some of the trees slows the rate at which leaves fill the pools. Each year some willows are pollarded and a few other trees thinned to increase the lifespan of the trees. The reedbeds need to be protected from encroaching scrub and trees, and are cut in rotation to keep the water channels open. Having a path with a firm surface encourages visitors not to stray onto places where vulnerable plants are growing. Invasive non-native species such as snowberry, rhododendron and Japanese knotweed are controlled to protect the native species.

HOW TO GET THERE

Kennington Pools [SP520032]

Kennington, south of Oxford. The nearest car park is Redbridge Park and Ride: walk left along Abingdon Road, and take the first left down Kennington Road. The entrance to Kennington Pools is on your left, opposite the entrance to Upper Road on the right. If heading clockwise on the Oxford ring road, leave the southern bypass (A4074) and head south when joining Kennington Road. If heading anticlockwise around the ring road, leave the southern bypass (A4074) onto Abingdon Road (towards the Redbridge Park and Ride). Take the first right down Kennington Road. The site entrance is on your left.

www.ocv.org.uk/sites.php?id=139

Kennington Pools

40 Kennington Meadows

Kennington flood meadows are used for grazing and are popular for riverside picnics, fishing and swimming. They were donated for conservation in 1972, relatively early in the movement, to save flood meadows from gravel extraction. The Thames Path between Sandford Lock and Iffley crosses the meadows. Footpaths lead down to Sandford Pools and islands that have been left to be wildlife friendly.

Oxford Preservation Society Marker in Kennington Meadows

HOW TO GET THERE

Simon's Land [SPSP528025]

Heyford Lane, Littlemore, Oxford. Travelling by road from Littlemore to Sandford-on-Thames, Heyford Lane is on the right, immediately after a bridge crossing the A4074. Simon's Land is on an S bend, about 200 yards after the lane narrows and has a rougher surface. There is no parking at the entrance; it is better to park by the roadside before the lane narrows.

www.oxfordpreservation.org.uk/land/simonsland.php

41 Simon's Land

Simon's Land and the nearby Heyford Meadow are on the eastern bank of the Thames in Littlemore. They are owned by the Oxford Preservation Society and have been improved for visitors and wildlife. Simon's Land first opened in 2011. It is a small wooded area, overlooking the Thames where it bends round Rose Island, and has a good view of Kennington Meadows. It is a quiet place to sit on a summer day. The nearest refreshments are at pubs in Littlemore and Sandford.

The view from Simon's Land across to Kennington Meadows

HOW TO GET THERE

Kennington Meadows [SP525025]

Kennington Meadows, south of Oxford. The Thames Path runs through the meadows, and National Cycle Network Route 5 runs between the north end of the meadows and the railway line. Mooring is allowed by the meadow above Sandford Lock, beyond the waiting place for the lock. The nearest car park is at the lower end of Sandford Lane at the south end of Kennington. The nearest road is in Kennington, by the Tandem Pub, via a path and railway footbridge [SP525025].

➤ HOW TO GET THERE

Heyford Meadow [SP532023]

Heyford Lane, Littlemore, Oxford. When travelling from Littlemore to Sandford-on-Thames, Heyford Lane is on the right, immediately after a bridge crossing the A4074. Heyford Meadow is reached by walking down Broadhurst Gardens. If coming by bus, you take the Thames Travel 105/106 from Oxford Centre to Littlemore and Sandford. The Thames Path is on the opposite side of the river, reached by walking to Sandford Lock about a mile away. You can moor on the meadow above Sandford Lock.

www.oxfordpreservation.org.uk/land/heyfordmeadows.php

42 Heyford Meadow

Heyford Meadow has been restored, with paths across the grassland and boardwalks through the marsh. The old trees attract woodpeckers, and give buzzards somewhere to roost. There is also a small scrape with a birdwatching screen. For children, there is a little playground outside one of the entrances. In July there is a mass of meadowsweet.

43 Thrupp Lake, Radley

Thrupp Lake is a former gravel pit, saved from becoming a waste disposal site by the local community. The reserve has been much improved recently with two bird hides, a boardwalk and a very good information board. In spring look for common spotted orchids, and in summer look out for butterflies and other insects. All year round, there are plenty of water birds. The entrance and bird hide are suitable for wheelchairs, but parking is not easy. The bird hide is also a shelter and a place to sit and rest. There is an interesting circular walk of about a mile around the lake. Volunteers work at the site once a month (contact the Earth Trust, who manage the reserve).

Meadowsweet at Heyford Meadow

Thrupp Lake

▶ HOW TO GET THERE

Thrupp Lake [SU520978]

Thrupp Lane, Radley OX14 3NG. There is no car park nearby, but you may find a space beside the lake. However, go carefully as heavy lorries use adjacent sites. This is a reserve best reached by cycling or walking along National Cycle Network Route 5 (Didcot to Oxford). If you are walking the Thames Path, you will find this cycle route in Barton Fields (see page 80). Radley train station is about a mile away. You can moor above and below Abingdon Lock – about a mile away.

www.earthtrust.org.uk/Places/ThruppLake/ThruppLake_Info.aspx

Abbey at Abingdon

44 Abingdon Community Woodland

HOW TO GET THERE

Abingdon Community Woodland [SU520968]

Lies beside the Thames Path between Abingdon and Radley, between the railway bridge across the river and Abingdon. It is not easily accessed by car. Mooring is possible along the riverbank.

This is a wood with alder trees planted beside the Thames, and there are meadows among the trees and places to picnic. Although the trees are planted in straight lines, as the wood matures the appearance is becoming more natural. It is open all the time, but there are no facilities apart from some seating.

Conservation has been strong in Abingdon, as shown by the places described here. There is an equal care of buildings for visitors to admire – from the archways of the former abbey buildings, through the council chambers and the market place, to the atmosphere around St Helen's Church. From St Helen's Church there is a lovely path beside the River Ock on the south side of the town.

45 Abbey Fishponds

Abbey Fishponds is a community nature reserve that lies between Radley Road and Audlett Drive in the northern suburbs of Abingdon, providing a lovely green space in the midst of all the housing constructed over the last 30 years.

Once a medieval fish farm, the reserve is a small valley with a stream that runs into the Thames about a mile away. There is a large reedbed on the eastern side, and grassy spaces and scrub along the west side of the stream. In spring there are southern marsh orchids, which appear after the grass has been cut. Marsh marigolds and yellow iris grow in the wetter areas, and ragged robin, devil's-bit scabious and valerian are reminders that this was once open countryside. The reedbeds and surrounding bushes attract reed buntings and sedge warblers, and in the summer there are abundant damselflies.

The reserve is open at all times. It is managed by the Berks, Bucks & Oxon Wildlife Trust (BBOWT), with the help of local volunteers. Apart from notice boards at the entrances into the reserve, there are no facilities such as seats or information boards. Dogs must be kept on leads at all times.

HOW TO GET THERE

Abbey Fishponds OX14 3TN [SU510981]

Radley Road, Abingdon. There are two entrances in Radley Road where there is some street parking, and also two paths from Audlett Drive, where there are car parks at the White Horse Leisure Centre OX14 3PJ [SU514 976] and at Barrow Hills [SU515983]. If walking from the town centre, the best route is to start along the Thames Path to Barton Fields Reserve. Take National Cycle Network Route 5 to the far end of the reserve, and look for a gate through to the modern industrial estate. Immediately across the road is a path (cycling also permitted) around the Leisure Centre to Audlett Drive. Cross Audlett Drive, turn right, and walk for 100 yards to a path beside a small stream. This path is a way into the reserve, about a mile from the Thames Path. You can moor above and below Abingdon Lock, about a mile away. Buses run from the centre of Abingdon along Radley Road.

www.bbowt.org.uk

Abbey Fishponds

Seat at Barton Fields

46 Barton Fields

HOW TO GET THERE

Barton Fields [SU512973]

Barton Lane, Abingdon. This reserve can be reached from the car park for Abbey Meadow by following the Thames Path and the signs for National Cycle Network Route 5, or by finding Barton Lane (signposted as 'scientific park'), which is off Audlett Road in Abingdon.

www.abnats.org.uk

Barton Fields is a Local Nature Reserve next to Abbey Meadows near the centre of Abingdon. It is within easy walking and cycling distance of the town centre. Bordering the Thames, the site consists of a diverse range of habitats including dry grassland, a wildflower meadow, willow carr and wetlands, and is home to a diverse range of flora and fauna. The site has been managed by members of the Abingdon Naturalists Society since 1999 and was designated as a Jubilee Wildlife Site in 2003. The volunteers have seeded the wildflower meadow, cut overgrown vegetation, dug ponds and planted trees.

Within walking and easy cycling distance of Barton Fields are Abbey Fishponds (see page 79 for directions), Thrupp Lake (along National Cycle Network Route 5) and Andersey Island (across Abingdon Lock). Abingdon Community Woodland is about 1½ miles along the Thames Path going upstream towards Oxford.

47 Andersey Island

Andersey Island lies between the Thames and the Swift Ditch. The latter was once the navigable stream and has the remains of an early pound lock with a board explaining the way the lock worked. Here are flood meadows that have been left to go wild and plantations of young woodland. There is a good circular walk from the car parks by Abingdon Bridge, where there are information boards.

HOW TO GET THERE

Andersey Island [SU508981]

On the southeast side of Abingdon. From Abingdon Bridge, walk along the Thames Path to Abingdon Lock. Stay on the same side of the river, and continue on the path past the watering point for boats, where you will reach wide meadows where grass grows tall. There are paths with no signposts, but finding one's way is not difficult in the open space. There is another path from Rye Farm car park, on the Culham Road, which is the best place to park. Mooring is permitted above and below Abingdon Lock and along the riverbank at the upper end of the island.

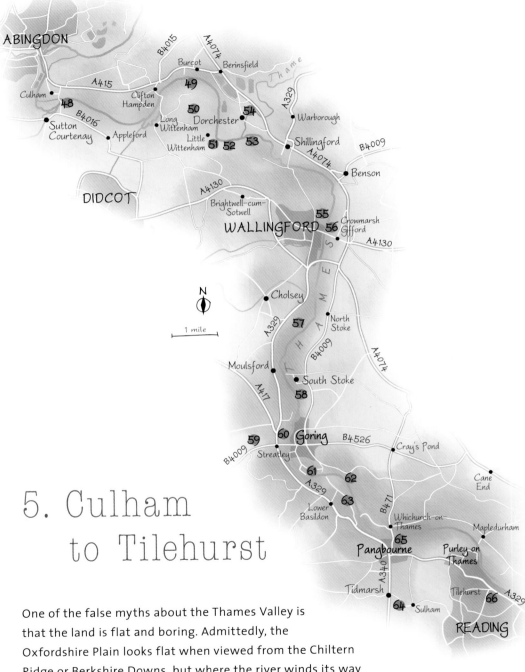

ABINGDON

B4015
A4074

Burcot
Berinsfield

Thame

A415
Culham
Clifton
Hampden
48
B4016
Sutton
Courtenay
Appleford
Long
Wittenham
Little
Wittenham

49

50
Dorchester
54
Warborough

A329

51 52 53
Shillingford

B4009

A4074
Benson

DIDCOT

A4130

Brightwell-cum-
Sotwell

55
WALLINGFORD **56**
Crowmarsh
Gifford

A4130

N

THAMES

Cholsey

1 mile

A329
57
North
Stoke

B4009
A4074

Moulsford
A417
South Stoke
58

59
60 Goring
B4526
Cray's Pond

B4009
Streatley

Cane
End

61
A329
62

63
Lower
Basildon
B471
Whichurch-on-
Thames
Mapledurham

65
Pangbourne
Purley-on-
Thames

A340
Tidmarsh
64
Sulham
Tilehurst **66** A329

READING

5. Culham
to Tilehurst

One of the false myths about the Thames Valley is
that the land is flat and boring. Admittedly, the
Oxfordshire Plain looks flat when viewed from the Chiltern
Ridge or Berkshire Downs, but where the river winds its way
through the Chilterns, the steep valley sides are dramatic.
The wooded hillsides make a pleasing contrast to the grassy
waterside meadows, enriching the variety of habitats.

View from Wittenham Clumps

48 Sutton Pools

At Sutton Courtney, there is a cluster of weir pools lying between four islands that are linked by a footpath over the weirs. The largest island is a meadow that is the land between the Culham Cut to the lock and the original course of the river that is now the weir stream. The meadow has public access, and a path around its perimeter makes a pleasant 2 mile walk. The pools below the weirs are used for fishing, canoeing and picnics – look out for birds that compete for the fish; cormorants, herons, goosanders and kingfishers. There are good pubs in Culham and Sutton Courtney.

HOW TO GET THERE

Sutton Pools [SU508950]

The pools and meadow can be reached by walking from Sutton Courtney, near Abingdon. By car, the easier access is to use the small car park near Culham Lock; this is beside the road between the A415 at Culham and the B4016 at Sutton Courtney. From the car park, walk across the bridge over the lock cut, and enter the meadow on the right (west) side, where there is a notice that describes the meadow. The Thames Path runs along Culham Lock Cut and is reached via a footbridge; this is close to a mooring in Culham Lock Cut.

HOW TO GET THERE

Clifton Meadow [SU568945]

You get to this area via the meadow between Day's Lock and Clifton Hampden – reached by walking along the Thames Path, which runs through it. There is an information board that tells you when you are at the meadow. Parking is possible at a layby on the Clifton Hampden side of the bridge, and at the Barley Mow pub. The Thames Path crosses the river on Clifton Bridge, but this section of the Thames Path is not suitable for cycling. There is a mooring site above Clifton Bridge, on the Clifton Hampden bank.

www.earthtrust.org.uk

49 Clifton Meadow

Clifton Meadow is a flood meadow that lives up to its name because a boardwalk is needed to cross it in winter. In some parts it is so wet that reeds are replacing the rough grass. These places attract waders in winter and are the hunting ground for herons looking for frogs. A visit to Clifton Meadow could be combined with Neptune and Paradise Woods, by using a footpath between Long Wittenham and the meadow. The nearest pub is the Barley Mow, featured in Jerome K. Jerome's *Three Men in a Boat*, on the Wittenham side of Clifton Bridge.

Sutton Pools

Notice at Neptune Wood

Blackthorn blossom

HOW TO GET THERE

Paradise Wood and Neptune Wood [SU554939]

The woods are reached from a lane between Long Wittenham and Little Wittenham, South Oxfordshire. There is a good car park. From the Thames Path you can either walk from Day's Lock through Little Wittenham to a gateway into the meadows beside the woods [SU563933], or find the footpath near Clifton Meadow (see below). Mooring is allowed above Day's Lock. National Cycle Network Route 5 passes through Long Wittenham and Little Wittenham.

www.earthtrust.org.uk

50

Paradise Wood and Neptune Wood

Preserving and creating woodland is one of the main purposes of the Earth Trust, which owns this reserve. Neptune Wood has broad-leaved trees, planted in 2005 on the 200th anniversary of the Battle of Trafalgar. Paradise Wood, though, is older. There are good walks around the woods, an area of ponds, and a meadow beside the lane. There is an interesting link to the British Navy in the 18th and early 19th centuries, when the docks along the Thames were very important. This is explained on good information boards with maps.

The Earth Trust Centre in Little Wittenham has a café, about a mile away across some meadows. Please check the opening times and arrangements at the Earth Trust website. There are several pubs in Long Wittenham. Also close by are Wittenham Clumps and Little Wittenham Wood.

51 Wittenham Clumps

At the Wittenham Clumps you'll find the Round Hill and Castle Hill, with ancient fortifications. Both hilltops are now wooded, and surrounded by meadows. The Round Hill has wonderful views along the Thames towards Buscot, and the meadows are full of downland wildflowers in summer. The Earth Trust has volunteer activities and a centre with teaching space nearby. There is a network of paths around the Clumps, and between the Clumps and Little Wittenham Wood.

HOW TO GET THERE

Wittenham Clumps and Little Wittenham Wood [SU567924]

Little Wittenham, Oxfordshire. There is a car park by the road between Little Wittenham and Brightwell-cum-Sotwell [SU567924]. Parking is also possible on the side of the road near Little Wittenham Church [SU566934]. Wittenham Clumps is on National Cycle Network Route 5. Mooring is permissible above Day's Lock. Didcot is the nearest train station (also on NCN5).

www.earthtrust.org.uk

Wittenham Clumps

*Logs make winter quarters
for small creatures in
Little Wittenham Wood*

Did you know...
There are at least 383
bridges across, and
25 tunnels under,
the Thames and its
subsidiary channels.

52 Little Wittenham Wood

Little Wittenham Wood stretches along the river with a variety of broad-leaved trees. A bird hide provides a quiet spot to observe the river – look out for kingfishers and herons. There are several trails around the wood. Springs in the hillside run into ponds and boggy areas. A bridleway goes straight through the wood and forms part of the circular walk on pages 90-91.

53 North Farm

North Farm was acquired by the Earth Trust to create a new wetlands reserve, and there are plans to make backwaters and shallow channels to encourage fish to spawn and amphibians to multiply. Part of the concept is to demonstrate the value of wetlands in controlling floods. At present the only parts of the reserve that can be visited are the bridleway and the permissive path described in the circular walk (pages 90-91), but in future there will be much more to see when the plans come to fruition.

Little Wittenham ···· Shillingford ···· Day's Lock ···· Little Wittenham

Dorchester Abbey from North Farm

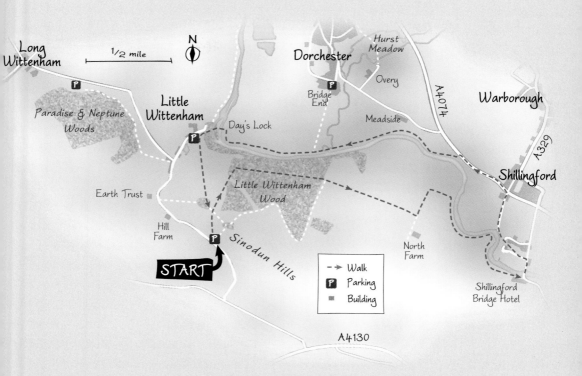

7 MILES Starting at one of the car parks at Little Wittenham and Wittenham Clumps, use the maps on the information boards to find your way into Little Wittenham Wood. In the wood, take the bridleway that runs parallel to the river, to emerge at a field on the far side. Continue straight along the bridleway until you see a permissive footpath sign on the left that takes you to the river. It reaches the riverbank where there was once a ferry. From this point there is a riverside path – the old towpath – down to Shillingford Bridge, where there is a riverside hotel with visitors' moorings. There are pubs in Shillingford if you want a choice of eating places. Cross Shillingford Bridge and look for the signs for the Thames Path on the left-hand side. The Path goes along a private driveway for about 50 yards, before veering to the right. It comes to a lane where there is an old wharf and slipway. You go up this lane to the main A4074 road. Unfortunately there is no alternative but to walk beside this road for a third of a mile until you see a Thames Path sign and stile into a riverside meadow. From here the Thames Path leads to Day's Lock. Just before the lock, cross the river on the 'Poohsticks' bridge, where the international Poohsticks championships are held each spring, to get back to Little Wittenham and the Clumps where you started. The walk can be extended by diverting to Hurst Water Meadow or Paradise and Neptune Woods.

54 Hurst Water Meadow

 HOW TO GET THERE

Hurst Water Meadow
[SU583942]

Dorchester-on-Thames, Oxon. There is a free car park at Bridge End, near Dorchester Abbey. From the car park, walk along the road over the bridge, leaving Dorchester behind you, until you come to a lane to Overy Farm. At the end of this lane you will find a footpath that takes you across the millstream and into Hurst Water Meadow; the meadow is about a mile from the Thames Path, which can be reached by a footpath on the west side of the River Thame from the car park at Bridge End. Buses from Oxford to Wallingford and Reading stop at Dorchester (some on the bypass and others in the village).

www.hurst-water-meadow.co.uk

This is an ancient water meadow on an island between the Thame and Overy Millstream, and it is a fine example of local community action to conserve a wildlife habitat. More than 60 plant species have been recorded, including a large oak and a magnificent black poplar tree. Water voles, kingfishers and herons are seen around the edges of the meadow. Volunteers are invited to help with managing the site.

Although there are limited facilities on site, there are public toilets by the car park, and a variety of places to eat in Dorchester. The Abbey is well worth visiting.

Hurst Water Meadow with Dorchester Abbey in the background

55 Wallingford Castle Meadows

Wallingford Castle was a large and important fortification until the Civil War when it was one of many buildings destroyed by the Parliamentary Army. The ditches remain and several parts of the castle walls are still standing. Beyond the formal gardens, near the entrance from Wallingford town centre, there is a large meadow which is managed to encourage wildflowers. This meadow has most of the outer defences of the castle, which have saved it from being ploughed and intensively cultivated. The grasses and flowers are as they must have been five centuries ago. A second meadow below the Castle Meadow goes down towards the river, and can flood after heavy rain. For nature studies there are copses and a small pond.

 HOW TO GET THERE

Wallingford Castle Meadows [SU607896]

The castle is on the north side of the town, with an entrance in Castle Street. It is an easy walk from the riverside car park. The Thames Path is very close. There are good bus services to Wallingford from Oxford and Reading, and National Cycle Network Route 5 goes through Wallingford. Good moorings are available above Wallingford Bridge.

www.earthtrust.org.uk

Defensive ditches at Wallingford Castle Meadows

56 Wallingford Riverside Meadow

Wallingford features a classic riverside meadow with lots of common wildflowers and bushes. It exists for people to enjoy a green space by the river, with a recreation centre, swimming pool and camping site nearby.

 HOW TO GET THERE

Wallingford Riverside Meadow [SU612874]

The meadow is by Wallingford Bridge on the Crowmarsh (east) side of the river. The car park is on the upstream, north side of the bridge. The Thames Path is very close, and there are good bus services to Wallingford from Oxford and Reading. National Cycle Network Route 5 goes through Wallingford. Good moorings are available above Wallingford Bridge.

www.earthtrust.org.uk

Wallingford Riverside Meadow

57 Cholsey Marsh

Cholsey Marsh is a long stretch of riverside meadow with marshes and scrub, which has been protected from housing developments on the site of the former Fairmile Hospital. There are Loddon lilies in spring, warblers and reed buntings in summer, and waders in the autumn – the marshy area has been fenced off to allow it to be grazed. There is a lot of space beside the Thames Path, with thickets of blackthorn and a grassy area, where there is a seat so walkers can rest.

HOW TO GET THERE

Cholsey Marsh [SU601855]

Ferry Lane, off the A329, Cholsey OX10 9HH. There is limited roadside parking near the reserve. The Thames Path runs through the marsh, and mooring is permitted along the bank. There is a bus and train service to Cholsey.

www.bbowt.org.uk

Cholsey Marsh

Did you know...
Otters and water voles in the Thames are increasing while European eels are declining.

58 Withymead Nature Reserve

 HOW TO GET THERE

Withymead Nature Reserve [SU601828]

Bridle Way, Goring-on-Thames, Oxfordshire RG8 OHS. Open by prior arrangement (tel: 01491 872 265) from April to September, and on Sundays and Bank Holidays in April and May, 11am to 4pm. If travelling by car, turn off the B4009 north of Goring into a lane signposted to the Leatherne Bottle and Goring Sailing Club. Withymead is on the left after the sailing club and several large houses. If coming by train you go via Goring and Streatley Station and walk to Cleeve, then continue along the Ridgeway Path. Cycling is permitted where the Ridgeway Path is a designated bridleway. If arriving by boat you need to moor below Goring Lock and walk to Cleeve, as above.

www.withymead.co.uk

Withymead is a 23 acre nature reserve with reed fens, wet woodland and an island. It has masses of Loddon lilies, and the reserve is open on Sundays and bank holidays in April and May so that people can enjoy the spectacle. A century ago, the site was a boatyard for a company that became the famous Saunders and Roe, builders of flying boats on the Solent. Some sheds, slipways and an old workers cottage remain as evidence of its history.

In addition to the Loddon lilies, the reserve has a colony of Desmoulin's whorl snails (a tiny snail that lives on reeds and other tall water plants) that is best seen in summer.

The reserve is developing a visitor centre with displays to show the ecology and history of the site; new courses for adults and a wildlife club for children started in 2012. The reserve has an active band of local volunteers.

Dogs are not permitted.

A way through the marsh at Withymead

Lardon Chase

59

Lardon Chase, the Holies and Lough Down

Lardon Chase, the Holies and Lough Down are a combination of National Trust properties, consisting of 67 acres of wildlife habitat. The grassy chalk hillside has stunning views over the Goring Gap and the River Thames. The Ridgeway National Trail passes close by.

The insects include mining bees, wasps and wolf spiders and a wide range of butterflies (chalkhill blue, grizzled and dingy skippers). The flowers are autumn gentian, clustered bellflower, blue fleabane, vervain, common rock-rose, horseshoe vetch and a good population of orchids.

There is a good walk starting at the car park by Lardon Chase. Walk along the ridge of Lardon Chase in a northeasterly direction, down the hill into Streatley, past the Bull Inn at the crossroads, continue on the main road for a short distance past the YHA Hostel, take a footpath (not well signposted) up some steps and a steep path through woodland. Towards the top of the path, take a right turn along a path that winds down and up through beech woodland to find a path that leads through the Holies to the car park where you started – a distance of 2 miles.

HOW TO GET THERE

Lardon Chase, the Holies and Lough Down [SU583807]

Take the narrow B4009 road from the crossroads in Streatley (traffic lights) up a steep hill to the Berkshire Downs. At the top of the hill there is a small National Trust car park where a footpath crosses the road.

www.wildaboutbritain.co.uk/lardon-chase-hollies-lough-down
www.nationaltrail.co.uk/ridgeway/siteasp?PageId=68&SiteId=140&c=7

60 Streatley Meadow

Did you know...
Thames islands are known as Aits or Eyots and are mostly formed by dividing streams, silt and sedimentation deposits.

Streatley Meadow became a conservation area in 2011, to preserve an area of grassland in the centre of the village for public events, such as the May Fair, and for people to walk and enjoy views of the church and river. The meadow is entered by a metal kissing gate from the road that goes from the crossroads to Goring. If you walk across the meadow you will find a wooden gate into a second meadow. Crossing this, a third gate goes into a recreation ground with a children's playground. Another footpath leads from this recreation ground to the village, reaching the road again by the Swan Hotel near the bridge.

61 Little Meadow, Goring

 HOW TO GET THERE

Little Meadow, Goring
[SU604796]

Start at the Thames Path in Goring and follow the signs towards Pangbourne, Whitchurch and Reading. Little Meadow is the field on the west side of the Gatehouse railway viaduct, near Goring.

Little Meadow is on the Thames Path between Hartslock and Goring, on the west side of the railway bridge across the river (Gatehampton Viaduct). It is a small reserve created by the Goring and Streatley Environment Group and is managed as a traditional hay meadow to encourage wildflowers. There is a good example of willow coppicing, and a seat where you can sit and watch the river. The Thames Path runs through the meadow, so it is open at all times; this reserve is most likely to be visited on the way to Hartslock Meadow. The footpath between Little Meadow and Goring is muddy in some places, making it difficult for those using pushchairs. The proper cycle path between Goring and Reading takes a different route from the Thames Path to the other side of the Gatehampton Viaduct. Cafés, toilets, car park, trains and buses can be found at Goring.

62 Hartslock Meadow

This is a chalk hillside with lovely views of the river and Berkshire Downs. Having climbed the steep slope up from the river, you will want to sit on the seat and admire the view. The reserve is best known for the orchids in April and May – the rare monkey orchids are individually marked. The fields in which the orchids are growing have marked pathways so you can see the orchids without trampling on them. Other orchids include the common spotted orchid, bee orchid and pyramidal orchid. Large patches of cowslips are another springtime attraction of this site – well worth the climb up the hill. Later in the summer, the hillside smells beautiful, with mauve marjoram flowers. The Berks, Bucks & Oxon Wildlife Trust (BBOWT) have volunteer activities at this reserve.

HOW TO GET THERE

Hartslock Meadow [SU616795]

Near Goring-on-Thames. There is no parking nearby, so if you are coming by car you can park in Goring and walk along the Thames Path, going downstream. If coming by train, take the small road outside Goring Station towards Gatehampton, then look for signs for a bridleway at SU607802. This will bring you to the Thames Path. This is also the best route for cyclists, as it avoids cycling through muddy sections of the Thames Path where cycling is not officially permitted. The Thames Path runs below the meadow. The entrance is not signposted, but is above the Thames Path, SU615794, at the edge of a wood. The Environment Agency has a 24 hour mooring site below Goring Lock; these moorings are beside the Thames Path.

www.hartslock.org.uk

View from Hartslock Meadow

63 Beale Park

The River Thames connects to Beale Park through a natural meadow leading to the car park at the main entrance. Beale Park is a 350 acre reserve, which was converted from private farmland to the conservation of wildlife for public enjoyment in 1956 by Gilbert Beale. The park nurtures rare and endangered plant and animal species. For the Thames wildlife, it presents a good example of a functioning floodplain ecosystem, including a reedbed and wildflower meadow, clearly described on the information boards. These natural areas provide food and shelter for a wide range of plant, insect, bird and small mammal species. They are accessible to the public to view, with pushchair and

Marsh marigolds

Taking time out by
the river at Beale Park

Tortoiseshell butterfly

wheelchair access pathways and a raised boardwalk.

An Education Room welcomes hundreds of schoolchildren each year and is open to visitors to learn about the animals, plant species and historic discoveries at the park.

There is a bird hide between the River Thames and the park at the outer edge of the lake system. Children will enjoy the adventure playground, Little Tikes Play Area, the paddling pool, sandpit, and a train ride through the park. There are five picnic areas, with grass, shade and seating. Because of the rare animals, dogs and other pets are not allowed, except for assistance dogs.

Beale Park volunteer opportunities include hands-on with nature outdoor activities, such as pond dipping, building nesting boxes and bug hotels; and species monitoring.

What to look for in the reedbed

» Phragmites reeds flourish in the shallow waters draining to the Thames and sustain many plant species such as meadow thistle, teasel, greater spearwort, vetches and morning glory. Bird life includes foraging bittern, marsh harrier, bearded tit, and Savi's warbler. Animal life can include water vole, otter, harvest mice and shrew. Insect life includes reed leopard moth, Fern's wainscot moth, damselflies, dragonflies and water boatman.

What to look for in the wildflower meadow

» The perennial meadow includes more than 12 grass species, including sweet verral, crested dogstail and smooth meadow grass, and 25 other seed plants, including the field poppy, wild carrot, cowslip, corn marigold and foxglove.

🔵 HOW TO GET THERE

Beale Park Wildlife Park and Gardens [SU618783]

Lower Basildon, Reading, Berkshire RG8 9NH. Situated on the A329, just outside Pangbourne, signposted from Junction 12 of the M4 (Theale). The park is open daily from 14 February to 31 October (admission fees apply). The Thames Path from Pangbourne to Goring goes on the other side of the river, via Whitchurch. The former towpath runs between the river and Beale Park, with an entrance from the riverside. There are overnight moorings beside this path. If travelling by train, Pangbourne station is a mile away. If coming by bus, it is bus service 133, operated by Thames Travel, from Reading Station and Goring Station (tel: 01491 837 988). There is also a passenger boat service from Reading.

www.bealepark.co.uk

Foxgloves — a sign of ancient woodland at Moor Copse

64 Moor Copse

 **HOW TO GET THERE**

Moor Copse [SU633738]

By the A340 road, between Theale and Pangbourne. The Thames Path is about 2 miles away at Pangbourne. There is a footpath from the Moors in Pangbourne that goes via Tidmarsh Mill on the River Pang to Moor Copse. Pangbourne Station is 2 miles away. The nearest mooring is at Pangbourne Meadow.

www.moorcopse.org.uk

Moor Copse is one of the jewels in the crown of the Berks, Bucks & Oxon Wildlife Trust (BBOWT). Although a bit more than a mile from the Thames, we could not resist including it in this book. The woods were bequeathed to BBOWT in 1975, and the meadows were added in 2006. A wildlife walk takes you round the reserve through three woods – Moor Copse, Hogmoor and Park – and two meadows. The River Pang flows through Moor Copse on its way to the Thames.

There are masses of bluebells in spring and fungi in autumn. Other spring flowers are wood anemones, primroses and dog violets. Trees are being planted to reduce the noise from the M4 motorway. Roe deer live among the trees and water voles are beside the River Pang. The water vole species is 'Ratty' from the Wind in the Willows, and the area is thought to have inspired Kenneth Grahame, who grew up in Cookham and lived in Pangbourne later in his life.

There are activities for volunteers for coppicing, thinning trees and stock watching, and a choice of cafés and pubs at Pangbourne, Tidmarsh and Theale. Other places nearby are Pangbourne Meadow and Beale Park.

65 Pangbourne Meadow

Pangbourne has a pleasant riverside meadow managed by the parish council and the National Trust. The reserve is mostly grassland, with reeds and scrub on the side that is away from the river. The alder trees by the river are a typical Thames species. It is open at all times and is popular for walks from the village, and the mown area of grass is good for picnics and games in summer. Near the entrance there is a playground on the inland (south) side where there are public toilets. The convenient moorings are often full at weekends in the summer. There is a wide choice of pubs and cafés in the village. You can walk beside the river to Beale Park (2 miles), but for a longer walk of 3 miles, a footpath beside the River Pang will take you to Tidmarsh and the Moor Copse reserve.

 HOW TO GET THERE

Pangbourne Meadow [SU643768]

Pangbourne, near Reading. From the main road in Pangbourne, the A329, take the B471 to Whitchurch. Before you reach Whitchurch Bridge, there is a car park on the right (east) side. The Thames Path runs through the meadow. Pangbourne Station is nearby. Buses from Reading run through the village. There is mooring (free for 24 hours) at the meadow.

66 McIlroy Park

McIlroy Park is on a hill, with great views over the Thames Valley. It is a Local Nature Reserve in the middle of an urban area. The sides of the hill are wooded, making this part of the West Reading Woodlands. There is a sunken ancient track – 'Gypsy Lane' – lined with beech trees, and Romany Lane bounds the eastern side. There are old chalk pits in the west woodland. The land was donated by William McIlroy who owned a department store in Reading and was Mayor of Reading.

 HOW TO GET THERE

McIlroy Park [SU677744]

Pottery Road, Tilehurst, Reading. There are no car parks, but there is often parking space at the end of Pottery Road which is one of the residential streets around the park. The Thames Path goes beside the river in Tilehurst, and it is possible to moor beside the bank here (although not many boats do). Public transport is via buses to Tilehurst, and the train station.

www.sssi.naturalengland.org.uk/special/lnr/lnr_details.asp?C=3&N=&ID=688

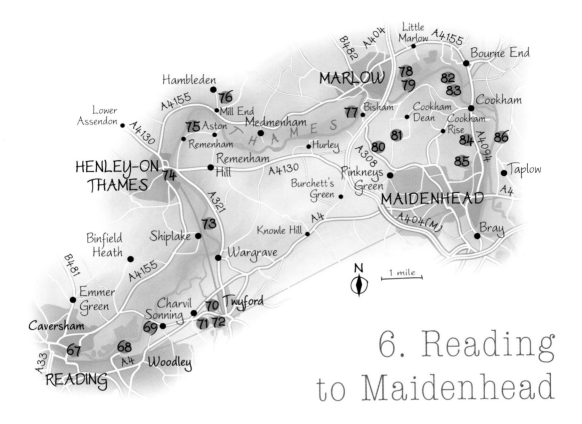

6. Reading to Maidenhead

The Thames from Reading to Maidenhead is what many people will think of when the name of the river is mentioned, with rowing clubs, elegant bridges and buildings, and green fields. During the regattas this part of the river is crowded, but away from the events there is plenty of green space and wildlife. The former gravel pits make havens for plants, insects and birds. The reserves at Charvil beside the Thames tributary, the Loddon, are popular with birdwatchers all year round. The flood meadows are fewer than upstream, and therefore even more precious. In this middle part of the non-tidal Thames, the River Thames Society has created its own reserve called Bondig Bank, near Marlow. Here, the grass verges and bushes on the bank are trimmed conservatively, balancing the need for human access with space for wildlife.

Fishing is a major interest for the whole length of the Thames. In the navigable non-tidal parts the predominant fish species are roach, dace, bream, chub, pike and perch. In the lakes, carp are popular with anglers. In the tributaries, brown trout and bullhead are present.

Sweet chestnut trees in Bisham Wood

Violets

Sculpture on View Island

67 View Island

HOW TO GET THERE

View Island [SU720743]

On the Caversham side of the river, below Reading Bridge. There is a car park on the Caversham (north) side of Reading Bridge. View Island is within a mile of Reading Station and town centre. There is a small landing stage on the island below the weir, suitable for canoes, and larger boats can moor by the park, upstream of Reading Bridge. The Thames Path and National Cycle Network Route 4 run on the other bank (south side) of the Thames.

View Island lies by the weir at Caversham Lock and next to a recreational park. The sound of water pouring over the weir masks the urban noises of Reading and its traffic, making this a wilderness haven. There was once a boatyard here, but there are no signs of this today. In the middle of the island, a space among the trees has been made into an open-air classroom, with log seats and a high canopy of leaves. There are wood sculptures and seats with views of the river, and local volunteers have cleared litter and brambles on the island.

Reading Borough Council has a Thames Parks Plan which aims to physically link the eight Thames Parks in Reading, including View Island. This plan will create a chain of high-value green spaces for wildlife and people.

Did you know...
There are 44 locks from the source of the Thames to Teddington Lock.

68 Thames Valley Park Nature Reserve

There is a large area of riverside meadows between the Thames and the modern Thames Valley Business Park. The eastern end of these meadows was once a waste tip for coal ash from Reading power station (now demolished). Restoration started in 1988, and was completed when Oracle, a major company in the Business Park, decided to manage the site as a nature reserve in 1994. The attractive ponds, surrounded by reeds and trees, have ducks and geese throughout the year, with some less common species such as gadwall in winter. The shrubs and reeds have warblers and buntings in summer. There are small platforms by some of the ponds that make good observation points. Grass snakes and adders have been reported. The large grass meadow makes this a great place for a family picnic.

> ▶ **HOW TO GET THERE**
>
> **Thames Valley Park Nature Reserve [SU746746]**
>
> Near the Thames Valley Business Park, Reading. There is a car park by Wokingham Waterside Centre (RG6 1PQ) or along the road entering the Business Park. If entering the large riverside meadows from the Reading end, walk east towards Sonning to find the reserve among the trees. It is close to the Thames Path and National Cycle Network Route 4. There is a public mooring for boats along the riverbank downstream from the reserve.

Lake at Thames Valley Park Nature Reserve

Ali's Pond

69 Ali's Pond, Sonning

Tucked away in a corner of a playing field is a sweet Local Nature Reserve called Ali's Pond, created in 1997. The pond has great crested newts, the meadow has wildflowers, and shrubs provide nesting areas for song birds. Pipistrelle bats use the bat boxes.

There are various activities (tree planting, haymaking and a survey) for volunteers advertised on the notice board at the reserve, and children from local schools and clubs use the reserve as an outdoor classroom.

For refreshment, there are attractive pubs in Sonning village. Ali's Pond and Thames Valley Park Nature Reserve are within walking distance of each other via the Thames Path.

70 Charvil Meadow

On the north side of the A3032, and the west side of the River Loddon, is Charvil Meadow, a good example of a Thames Valley flood meadow [SU780762]. The meadow is mostly visited by people who live in Charvil and can walk into it via Edward Road, Charvil, Reading RG10 9QS. There are paths across to a second entrance on the A4, where there is a parking space in a small layby nearby. For a longer walk, of about 3 miles, take the footpath opposite the A4 entrance to Charvil Meadow which goes northwards for a mile, to St Patrick's Stream. After crossing this side-stream of the Thames, turn left to walk through two fields and behind riverside houses. Re-cross St Patrick's Stream and turn left again to walk back to the A4 and Charvil along Milestone Avenue.

 HOW TO GET THERE

Ali's Pond [SU756753]

Sonning Lane, Sonning. Park in Pound Lane, Sonning, near the primary school, and walk westwards across the playing fields to a small meadow with hedges on three sides and a pond. From the Thames Path, walk from Sonning Bridge, through the churchyard, towards the entrance to Reading Blue Coat School. Opposite the school gate there is a small gate under a tree, from where a path crosses a field to Ali's Pond. National Cycle Network Route 5 passes through Sonning. Mooring is allowed beside the Thames Path above Sonning Lock.

www.sonning-pc.gov.uk/Village/Amenities/LNR/LNR.html

HOW TO GET THERE

Charvil Lakes [SU785758] and Loddon Nature Reserve [SU785758]

Charvil Lakes and the Loddon Nature Reserve are on the south side of the A3032 between Charvil and Twyford, Berkshire. The nearest public car park is in Polehampton Close off Twyford High Street. Loddon Nature Reserve is reached by walking along the High Street in Twyford towards Charvil, and taking a footpath on the left after 100 yards or so. This path crosses the River Loddon and enters the reserve. There is a second entrance at the back of the car park of the Waggon and Horses pub on the A3032; this entrance has an information map. To get to Charvil Lakes, walk along the pavement beside the A3032, past the Waggon and Horses pub, until you find a footpath on your left which takes you to the first of the Charvil Lakes. There is another entrance in Charvil. The train station at Twyford is within walking distance, and the reserve is near National Cycle Network Route 4. The Thames Path is not close, because it runs on the other (northern) side of the Thames between Sonning and Shiplake.

www.bbowt.org.uk

71 Charvil Lakes

As the crow flies, both Charvil and Loddon Lakes are within a mile of the Thames and so qualify to be included in this guide to the natural Thames. The short walk described on page 109, under Charvil Meadow, links them to the Thames. The lakes are large flooded gravel pits beside the River Loddon, which has two channels through the reserves. They offer birdwatchers a good chance of seeing waterfowl, including smew in winter. In spring and summer there are blackcaps, whitethroats and other warblers. The presence of kingfishers, herons and cormorants show that there are plenty of fish. There is a network of paths around Charvil Lakes, one of which runs under the railway line to more lakes on the southern side, where there is a heronry. There are no facilities on site, but Twyford and Charvil provide cafés, pubs and toilets.

72 Loddon Nature Reserve

Loddon Nature Reserve is situated on a lake next to the River Loddon. There is a public footpath between the Loddon and the east side of the lake, which continues southward under the railway, to Dinton Pastures, 3 miles away. Loddon Lake has islands used as nesting sites by geese, swans, ducks and terns. The wildlife walk is a path around the lake, with benches. These benches and the information board at the entrance by the Waggon and Horses pub are the only facilities on the reserve, but Twyford has a good selection of shops, cafés and pubs. The path to Dinton Pastures Country Park is an attractive walk beside the Loddon, and the park provides a café, information, toilets and a children's playground.

Loddon lilies beside
the River Loddon

73 Wargrave Marsh

⊙ HOW TO GET THERE

Wargrave Marsh [SU779808]

Willow Lane, Wargrave.
Willow Lane is on the A321
(Wargrave to Henley Road)
by Val Wyatt's boatyard. Go
past the sailing club and the
last house in the lane. Parking
is beside the road in the lane.
Look for a footpath after the
last house on the riverside,
and walk along it, beside the
river, to the northern tip of
the marsh. The moorings lie
beside this footpath. Buses
run along the A321, and
Wargrave Station is 1½ miles
away.

Wargrave Marsh is a reserve that is easily visited by boat, but is not so attractive for walkers or those coming by car. It is the lower (northern) end of a large island between the Thames and Hennerton backwater. Hennerton backwater, where kingfishers are often seen, is an example of the side-streams of the Thames, which are worth exploring by canoe where navigation is permitted. The marsh was an extensive area of fen and wet grassland, but scrub is gradually taking over the meadowland.

Towering above Wargrave Marsh are the chalk hills that have forced the Thames to make a large northern loop past Henley and Marlow to reach Maidenhead. Formerly the towpath ran along this side of the river, and remains as the path to the reserve and the Environment Agency mooring site. Nowadays, the Thames Path is on the opposite side of the river, and has to leave the riverside to go behind the houses in Lower Shiplake.

Ratty's Refuge

HOW TO GET THERE

Ratty's Refuge at the River and Rowing Museum [SU766821]

Mill Meadows, Henley RG9 1BF. The museum is well signposted from the centre of Henley, and has a large car park. The Thames Path is in front of the museum. The moorings by the meadows are free during the day (but are charged overnight). The station is next to the Mill Meadows.

www.rrm.co.uk

74 Ratty's Refuge at the River and Rowing Museum

Ratty's Refuge at the River and Rowing Museum is the smallest reserve in this guide. Designed as a wildlife garden for the Chelsea Flower Show, this is an example of how to encourage insects and frogs with just a small pond. It can be viewed from the terrace by the museum café. Inside the museum there is a display about the habitats and wildlife on the river.

The meadows in front of the museum have play areas and space for picnics. Upstream from the museum, towards Marsh Lock and its beautiful weir, there is a large open meadow, with corners where the plants are allowed to grow wild. This is a good space to explore, and it has its own car park, reached by Mill Lane, off the A4155 road on the Reading side of Henley.

Did you know...
There are more than 200 rowing clubs on the river.

Temple Island

75 Temple Meadow

A walk beside the river, across Henley Bridge and down beside the regatta course, will take you to Temple Meadow [SU773850]. The grass meadow opposite Temple Island is a designated Site of Special Scientific Interest (SSSI), but it is mown too much to have the best features of a natural flood meadow. A little further on, continuing along the Thames Path, you will see red kites wheeling in the sky over the river. The kites have a roost in the trees near Aston, which is a village you may want to visit for refreshment at the Flower Pot pub.

76 Hambleden Valley and Rodbed Wood

The Hambleden Valley is a good place to experience the Chiltern beech woods or watch the red kites that were reintroduced in England in this area. There is a circular walk from Mill End car park that goes through the pretty village of Hambleden, and through the woods; and this walk can be extended to 5½ miles to go to Medmenham Ferry and Rodbed Wood before returning along the riverbank to Mill End.

Rodbed Wood has a path through willows and alders standing in marsh. It is used for bird censuses: warblers in summer; redpoll and siskin in winter.

There are toilets and information about the Hambleden Valley walks at the car park at Mill End.

Reed bunting

● HOW TO GET THERE

Hambleden Valley [SU785853] and Rodbed Wood [SU803836]

Near the A4155 between Henley and Marlow. The best parking place is a proper car park on the lane between Mill End and Hambleden [SU785853]. There is also roadside parking at Medmenham Ferry. The Thames Path is on the opposite side of the river, but is accessible by crossing the weir at Hambleden Lock. Mooring is permitted at the riverside meadow next to Rodbed Wood. Buses go along the A4155, with stops in Mill End and Medmenham.

www.nationaltrail.co.uk/ ThamesPath/uploads/ Hambleden%20&%20 Medmenham%20Circular%20 Walk(1).pdf

Rodbed Wood

77 Bondig Bank

HOW TO GET THERE

Bondig Bank [SU847855]

Beside the river between Marlow and Temple Lock. There is a car park at Higginson Park, Marlow, and the Thames Path runs through the reserve. Mooring is available at Higginson Park. Bus and train services run to Marlow, 1½ miles away.

www.riverthamessociety.org.uk

This small section of riverbank is owned by the River Thames Society. It has been managed as a nature reserve for the last four years, and its small size stimulated the Society to look at other reserves along the Thames, to see how it fits into the bigger picture. The reeds and willows were grown to protect the banks and provide summer homes for warblers, the nettles are left for butterflies, and the hawthorn bushes and alders are nesting places for birds. The Thames Path running along Bondig Bank is a popular walk from Marlow, so the Society tries hard to keep it in good order.

There is a lovely view of Bisham Church and the land has historical links to Bisham Abbey.

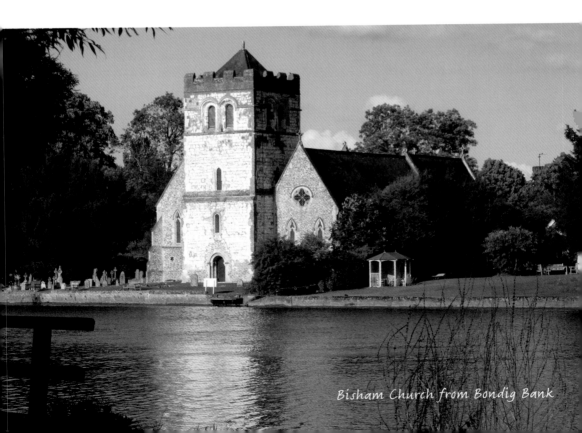

Bisham Church from Bondig Bank

78 Spade Oak Nature Reserve

Spade Oak Nature Reserve is a lake that was once a gravel pit, but the local community turned it into a nature reserve with support from the gravel company. It has a path on three sides that gives a good view of the birds; there is a protected peninsula for nesting and undisturbed roosting. It is also a popular fishing lake.

There are pubs in Little Marlow, and the Spade Oak Inn is close to the car park in Coldmoorholme Lane.

79 Spade Oak Meadow

Across the railway line from Spade Oak Nature Reserve is a large flood meadow, belonging to Buckinghamshire County Council and managed as public green space [SU883873]. Spade Oak Meadow is grazed in summer, but is very wet in winter. The Thames Path can be muddy here, which is a good reminder that it is a national trail through natural places, but not so user-friendly for those who want an easy walk beside the river. For visitors, the attraction is the area with seats overlooking a shallow bay with a sandy shore and a place to feed ducks, swans and geese on the river. For wheelchairs, Spade Oak Wharf is the best place to view the river.

 HOW TO GET THERE

Spade Oak Nature Reserve and Meadow [SU884875]

Coldmoorholme Lane, Little Marlow (off the A4155). The meadow is reached by crossing the railway line, and the reserve is entered by a footpath by the Spade Oak Inn and another path close to the church in Little Marlow. There is a car park in Coldmoorholme Lane between the meadow and the reserve. The train stations at Bourne End and Marlow are within walking distance, and buses run along the A4155 between Marlow and Bourne End. The Thames Path passes through Spade Oak Meadow. You can moor at Spade Oak Wharf.

www. littlemarlowparishcouncil. org.uk/Little-Marlow-Lakes-Countryside-Walks.pdf

Spade Oak Meadow

80 Bisham Woods

HOW TO GET THERE

Bisham Woods [SU850840 to SU870861]

Cookham to Pinkney Green, Berkshire. There are car parks at Winter Hill [SU870860], Cookham Dean Common (Winter Hill Lane) [SU861843], on the layby on the A404 [SU853850], and at Park Wood – up a track from the A308 [SU833842]. The Thames Path is on the closest point on the opposite side of the river, and the closest point is at Cock Marsh. Nearest moorings are at Cookham Meadow and Marlow.

These are extensive (378 acres) woodlands on the south bank of the Thames opposite Marlow. Collectively, they are called Bisham Woods, with interesting individual names: Park, Inkydown, Fultness, Quarry and Goulding's Woods. They are predominantly beech woods on a chalk soil. The river valley creates magnificent views over Bisham and Marlow to High Wycombe, and the plethora of paths, some on the maps, some not, will entice you to explore. There is a good circular walk following signposted paths from Cookham Dean Common to Winter's Hill, down towards the river, along to Fultness Wood, up to the bridleway by Park Wood and back to Cookham Dean (5 miles). At Fultness Wood, you pass a former icehouse (a chamber used for storing ice before refrigerators were invented).

Horse riding and cycling are permitted along the bridleways.

There are pubs in Cookham Dean.

Kenneth Grahame wrote *Wind in the Willows*, first published in 1908, while living in Cookham Dean, and Quarry Wood is thought to be the Wild Wood in the story.

Beeches in Bisham Woods

A bramble and a bee

81 Cookham Dean Common

On top of the ridge that forces the Thames northward is a large open common, Cookham Dean Common [SU862843], owned by the National Trust. The Trust also owns some of the village greens nearby. Set close to the Bisham Woods, Cock Marsh and Cookham Moor, this forms a very large protected area, which deserves to be better known. It is a charming area to explore along the footpaths and narrow lanes, before exploring Bisham Woods.

Dog rose

Cookham Dean Common

82 Cock Marsh

▶ HOW TO GET THERE

Cookham Moor [SU892854] and Cock Marsh [SU887867]

There is a car park (National Trust) at the southern end of Cookham Moor. The Thames Path runs through Cookham Moor and crosses the river at Bourne End railway bridge. Cock Marsh is reached by footpaths under the railway viaduct. National Cycle Network Route 50 from Maidenhead to High Wycombe passes by along the Green Way. There is a station in Cookham and buses run from Maidenhead. Mooring is permitted at Cookham Moor.

Cock Marsh is 46 acres of rough pasture with marshy areas and a chalk slope beneath Quarry Wood. It was common land which was secured for public use in 1934 when it was bought by the people of Cookham and given to the National Trust. Like other ancient riverside commons it has been used for grazing for centuries and is fertile soil. The name Cock probably derives from a Victorian archaeologist who excavated one of the Bronze Age burial mounds in the Marsh. Among the plants growing here is the rare brown galingale, a small sedge with brownish-purple flower spikes that mature into brown nutlike fruit.

There is a pub among the riverside bungalows and there is a path on the railway bridge to Bourne End.

From Cock Marsh you can explore Quarry Wood and climb Winter Hill for views over the Thames Valley.

Did you know...
Within the Thames River Basin there are 46 internationally designated Special Protection Areas and Areas of Conservation.

83 Cookham Moor

Cookham Moor is a flood meadow, which is popular with dog walkers and is good for picnics, and for watching boats on the river, especially during the Cookham Regatta. The grass is generally kept short, except at the north end of Cookham Moor, where there is an enclosed Schools Conservation area. There is a pond at the centre of this area, with a dipping platform. In spring, cowslips and cuckoo-flowers grow in this area amongst the rough grasses.

The Stanley Spencer Gallery and a selection of cafes and pubs are in Cookham. The Green Lane to Maidenhead runs from the south end of the moor.

Cookham Moor

84 Widbrook Common

Widbrook Common is grazing land owned by the National Trust beside the A4094 between Cookham and Maidenhead. It is bisected by a stream, called the White Brook (possibly a corruption of 'Wide Brook'), which flows into the Thames half a mile away. It can be visited by parking in a small layby beside the A4094 [SU898842]. From here you can look at the smaller section on the east of the road and walk round the larger western section. Widbrook Common may have been more popular in the past, because there is a faded notice about flying model aeroplanes, and local records describe children skating on a pond beside the White Brook. Today it is used by dog walkers and joggers. We suggest visiting the common as part of a circular walk from Cookham, via Green Way (see page 124). When on the common, enjoy the fine view of Cliveden Hotel across the river. If you look up, you will often see red kite hunting across the fields.

Widbrook Common in winter

85 North Town Moor

North Town Moor is a small remnant of the formerly extensive common land around Maidenhead that was lost to Victorian building. It is now an area of grassland with hedges and scrub. It is important as part of a green corridor, identified as the Green Way, that runs through the heart of Maidenhead. The small pond and stream give children the chance to look at aquatic plants and animals. By using the Green Way between Maidenhead and Cookham, and the Thames Path for a return journey, these reserves can be visited as part of a bike ride or a circular walk.

There are opportunities for volunteers to help conserve North Town Moor and nearby fields.

 HOW TO GET THERE

North Town Moor [SU890824]

North Town Moor is among the northern suburbs of Maidenhead SL6 7JR. From Maidenhead, take the Cookham Road, the B4447. After half a mile, turn right into Moor Lane, which leads you to North Town Moor (the name of the street and the grassland). There is a car park beside the pond at North Town Moor. It is on the Green Way path from Maidenhead to Cookham, and on National Cycle Network Route 50.

www.makespaceforlife.org

86 Cliveden

The woodlands at Cliveden are part of the large estate in this National Trust property. From the woodlands car park, there are three colour-coded walks of varying length (1½ to 3½ miles) and steepness. The woods extend down to the edge of the river where it is possible to moor a boat. The paths zig-zag up the steep side of the valley between beech trees and yew trees. From the top, at a lookout point, there are great views of the Berkshire Downs. There are wood sculptures and picnic places near the car park. From the woodlands you can walk into the formal gardens and find the café and other facilities by the main house.

The National Trust encourages volunteers to help with tree planting, pruning and clearing footpaths.

 HOW TO GET THERE

Cliveden [SU915851]

Cliveden Road, Taplow, South Buckinghamshire SL6 0JA. The car park for Cliveden Woodlands is about a mile from the main entrance on the road to Taplow [SU909832]. Mooring permitted (not free) at the Cliveden Estate. The Thames Path is on the opposite side of the river. To date, there is no foot or cycle path to Cliveden. The woodlands and gardens are open from 10am to 4pm in winter and until 5.30pm from spring to autumn.

www.nationaltrust.org.uk/ main/w-cliveden

Cookham ···· Maidenhead ···· Bray ····
Thames Path ···· Cookham

6–12 MILES

This walk can be shortened, but the longer version will take you to five nature reserves. It starts at the car park at Cookham Moor [SU892854]. Look at the signboard that describes the Green Way that is the foundation of this walk. Green Way goes to Maidenhead (about 3 miles) and Bray (5 miles). The other component of the walk is the Thames Path, for the return journey. Green Way and the Thames Path are well signposted, and this account focuses on a few tricky places.

Start on the south side of the road, where there are signs for the east and west routes of Green Way. Choose the east route because it will take you to Widbrook Common, the first reserve. At Widbrook Common [SU893838], you can rest on the wayside seat and look eastwards to Cliveden on the wooded ridge, which is above the Thames. Continuing on Green Way east, you cross a field to a gravel pit with a sailing club. Turn right and then left around the gravel pit and you come to a meadow which leads you to North Town Moor [SU890824], about 2 miles from Cookham. For the shortest walk, take a path going east to Summerleaze Road. At the far (east) end of Summerleaze Road, turn right and first left into

Bridge to North Town Moor

Ray Mill Road East which takes you to Boulter's Lock [SU903824] and the Thames Path for your return journey.

To enjoy a longer walk, continue along the Green Way by the pond at North Town Moor. This brings you to Town Moor [SU892818], a park near the centre of Maidenhead. A second shorter route is to veer leftwards (southeast) at Town Moor to get to Bridge Street where you turn left and go onto the Thames Path at Maidenhead Bridge.

The Green Way route leaves Town Moor on the west side after crossing a ditch, and twists and turns through central Maidenhead until it

runs beside a stream.

Green Way passes under the railway [SU891808], only a short distance from Maidenhead Station. This would be where to start if using public transport instead of parking at Cookham. It runs with National Cycle Network Route 4 from Maidenhead to Bray. Soon you reach Braywick Nature Park, where you can go straight along Green Way, or wander off to the left to find a path beside the Cut, a sizeable stream that was once navigable. At the far (southern) end of Braywick Park [SU895795], Green Way crosses Hibberts Lane, and veers diagonally left to the centre of the village of Bray. Walk through the centre to find Ferry Lane [SU903796]. A short distance down Ferry Lane, turn right into Monkey Island Lane. You may like to go further down Ferry Lane to the hotel/inn by the river, but there is no ferry service across to the Thames Path that is on the other (northeast) bank of the Thames.

Follow Monkey Island Lane towards the increasing sound of the M4. About 200 yards before the lane crosses the M4 motorway, there is a footpath on the left [SU909793]. This path is on the level of the motorway where it goes across the Thames. On the far side, there are steps down to the Thames Path. This is 5½ miles from the start (or longer if you have wandered around the reserves on the way). If you want to add a further mile to make an even longer route, stay on Monkey Island Lane to cross the M4 and find a footbridge across the Thames which is close to the northwest corner of Dorney Lake, yet another reserve, and return by the Thames Path.

The route back to Cookham along the Thames Path is well signposted. You pass

Bray Lock, which is often busy with boats on a summer's weekend. After passing beneath the magnificent railway bridge at Maidenhead, cross the Thames on Maidenhead road bridge. There is a small riverside park, and the Thames Path is diverted behind a block of flats before resuming its riverside route past Boulter's Lock, and opposite the upper entrance of the

Jubilee River and the whole of the Cliveden Estate. As you approach Cookham, the Thames Path is diverted away from the river behind houses and then emerges near the middle of the village. Depending on how you feel, you can stop for refreshment in one of the pubs or café, visit the Stanley Spencer Gallery, walk back to your car (completing nearly 12 miles) or go further along the Thames Path. The Thames Path winds around the church before emerging by the river. A short distance further beside the river, passing Cookham sailing club, and you are on Cookham Moor with a variety of paths across and around the meadows. If you still have the energy, walk further north to visit Cock Marsh before returning home.

Dramatic wood carving beside the Green Lane

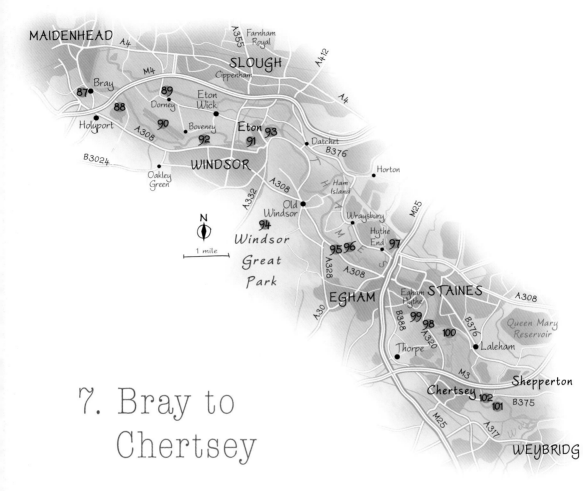

7. Bray to Chertsey

For Victorian and Edwardian Londoners, the Thames from Maidenhead to Runnymede was a favourite place for a day in the country. From Boulter's Lock at Maidenhead to Windsor, the river was crowded with skiffs, punts and steam launches. The area is still well served by the railways, so it remains a great place to visit. The land becomes more urban as the River Thames approaches London, and the river and Thames Path become more important as a green corridor or 'wildlife highway'. Runnymede and Windsor have significant historical interest as well as interesting wildlife. Braywick Park has lovely trees, in addition to being a great example of how wilderness habitats can be re-created amid parkland.

Braywick Park Nature Reserve

87 Braywick Park

⏵ HOW TO GET THERE

Braywick Park [SU895795]

Hibbert Road, off the A308, in Braywick, Maidenhead SL6 1UU. The car park has information boards. The Thames Path is on the opposite side of river, but can be reached by footpaths from central Maidenhead, via the Green Lane. The Green Lane is also a cycle route from central Maidenhead.

Maidenhead Station is the closest. Buses run to the park. There are moorings in Maidenhead and at Bray Marina, about 2 miles away. Open 7am to dusk.

www.rbwm.gov.uk

Braywick Park is the largest public open space in Maidenhead. In addition to good sports facilities, it has a 37 acre Local Nature Reserve and Braywick Nature Centre, used for environmental education within the borough. In the centre of the nature reserve is a large area of grassland and thickets that are raised above the surrounding woodlands and paths. There is a pond with reeds between this raised grassland and the more formal parkland near the entrance. A nature trail goes around the reserve beside the stream called the Cut, and round the northern end to join the Green Lane that runs from Cookham, through Maidenhead to Bray (see the circular walk in Chapter 6). The trees in the park are magnificent, and are cared for by volunteer tree wardens.

On the opposite side of the Cut to Braywick Park Local Nature Reserve is Bray Meadow, a designated Site of Special Scientific Interest (SSSI), located beside the B3028 [SU898801]. The meadow has a good variety of wildflowers, because this land has not been 'improved' by farming. However, there is no path across this site, and so no clear rights of public access.

Autumn sunshine in Braywick Park Nature Reserve

A peaceful scene at Bray Pits

88 Bray Pits

Between the A308 and the Thames, and to the south of the M4 motorway, lie a group of gravel pits used for sailing and other forms of recreation. Gravel is still being extracted from some pits.

The largest, Bray Lake, often has ducks (mallard and tufted), coots and a few great crested grebes in the corners away from the sailing. The most used footpath circles the main lake. There is a small Berks, Bucks & Oxon Wildlife Trust (BBOWT) reserve with a lake at the western end [SU905786]. Another lake between the Cut and the M4 has more waterfowl, as it is less disturbed by human visitors, but the noise from the M4 is intrusive.

There is another Site of Special Scientific Interest (SSSI), Bray Pennyroyal Field, which is so named because of the presence of a rare creeping plant, pennyroyal, which grows at the margin of the ponds. It is a field used as pasture for horses, and does not have public access. It is near the entrance to Bray Marina [SU915783].

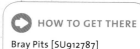 **HOW TO GET THERE**

Bray Pits [SU912787]

Monkey Island Lane, Bray (off the A308), signposted to Bray Marina. There is a car park at the sailing centre that is open during working hours, and space to park in the lane at other times. There are footpaths leading from the A308, of which the clearest is opposite Bray Cemetery [SU904785]. Monkey Island Lane is part of the Green Lane cycle path. The Thames Path is on the opposite side of the Thames and can be reached by crossing the Summerleaze footbridge near Monkey Island. Moorings are available for visitors at Bray Marina. The reserve is open at all times.

89 Jubilee River

HOW TO GET THERE

Jubilee River [SU905829 to SU976780]

There are three car parks, where the B3026 crosses the Jubilee River at Dorney [SU928795], where the A332 crosses near Eton [SU978782], and [SU914803] near Taplow. The riverside path is also National Cycle Network Route 61. The Thames Path and National Cycle Network Route 4 come close at Eton. The nearest station is at Taplow. The nearest moorings are at Windsor, Eton and Boveney. Open at all times.

www.jubileeriver.co.uk

The Jubilee River is an artificial channel designed to prevent flooding in Maidenhead and Windsor. Conservation started while the river was being built in 2000 and it has matured into a lovely stretch of water with reedbeds and islands.

The riverside path goes for 6 miles from Taplow to Eton and is suitable for cycling and wheelchairs. It links to a network of paths that cross the river by pretty footbridges.

In winter, it is a haven for waterfowl: mallards, widgeons, tufted ducks, teals, grebes, cormorants, herons, swans, and Canada and Egyptian geese.

Fishing is allowed, with permits. You can canoe on the Jubilee River, but you have to portage around the weirs.

There is a 10½ mile circular walk formed by the Jubilee River path, a path through Eton playing fields, the Thames Path up to Taplow, and back to the Jubilee River.

For refreshment, there are many cafés in Eton and Windsor. The Dorney Lake and Brocas Meadow are nearby.

Tufted ducks on the Jubilee River

90 Dorney Lake

Dorney rowing lakes were constructed by Eton College to international standards and were used for the Olympic Games in 2012. The land around the lakes is managed for wildlife as well as spectators. The area to the west of the practice lake (i.e. between the lakes and the Thames) is a nature reserve, and the hedges are laid in a traditional fashion. There are also two ponds and an information board about the archaeology of the area close to the cycle path on the east side of the lake.

Also of interest is a pretty little chapel, St Mary Magdalene, near the mooring site beside the Thames Path.

Dorney Lake

HOW TO GET THERE

Dorney Lake Rowing Centre [SU923790]

Off Court Lane, Boveney, South Bucks SL4 6QP. There is car parking within the rowing centre near the entrance (SU922789) and close to the main building (may be full during regattas). There is also another car park near Boveney Court Farm (SU938778). The Thames Path runs between the Thames and the Rowing Centre; the Rowing Centre can be reached by footpaths from the Jubilee River where there is car parking. The Environment Agency has a mooring site at the wharf near the southeast end of the lake [SU937774].

www.dorneylake.com

91 The Brocas

HOW TO GET THERE

The Brocas [SU967773]

Starting at Windsor Bridge, which crosses the Thames between the centre of Windsor and Eton, follow the signs for the Thames Path to Maidenhead. After a short lane, you will enter an open meadow beside the river. This is the Brocas. The Thames Path and National Cycle Network Route 4 run through the meadows. Overnight moorings can be found on the riverbank, and there is car parking in Eton. There are good train and bus services to Windsor.

The Brocas is the strange name for the riverside meadows, owned by Eton College, opposite the town of Windsor. The meadow closest to Eton is much used for summer activities including fairs, and is good for picnics. Further along, going towards Dorney Lake and Bray, the grass is longer, the bushes are thicker, and there is more chance of spotting interesting wildlife. It is open at all times and makes a pleasant part of the Thames Path and National Cycle Network Route 4.

The Brocas, Eton

*Sutherland Grange
Hay Meadow*

92 Sutherland Grange

Sutherland Grange was a house demolished long ago, but the park retains the name. The field on the western side of the park is known as Sutherland Grange Hay Meadow and has a huge variety of flowers and grasses. In summer there are lots of insects, including butterflies, beetles and moths, which provide food for a variety of birds nesting in the trees and hedges surrounding the site. This field has been designated a Local Nature Reserve. The rest of the park has mown grass that is suitable for ball games. Windsor Racecourse on the other side of the Mill Stream makes the whole green space larger.

 HOW TO GET THERE

Sutherland Grange [SU942771]

Maidenhead Road, Windsor. Parking is in a large layby on the A308. A bus service between Maidenhead and Windsor passes the Grange. Windsor has two stations, which are 2 miles away. The Thames Path is on the other side of the river.

www.rbwm.gov.uk

*Did you know...
From its source in Gloucestershire to Teddington in southwest London the Thames is non-tidal – a distance of 146 miles.*

The Cascade at Virginia Water

93 Windsor Home Park

Most of Windsor Home Park is typical parkland with mown grass and flowerbeds, but there is a corner by the river that is a wildlife habitat. On the Thames Path from Windsor Bridge towards Victoria Bridge (downstream), you will pass through a yard full of interesting wooden boats before arriving back at the river edge. You then enter the Home Park where the grass is left to grow long and nesting boxes have been put in the trees. This area makes the point that the Thames Path is itself a nature reserve for most of its length. It is all the more disappointing then that the Thames Path is diverted onto a pavement beside a main road (B3021) in Datchet, and away from the original towpath in Windsor Park.

94 Windsor Great Park

On the south side of Windsor Castle the Great Park stretches for 5 miles southwards to Virginia Water. It covers a large area (nearly 5,000 acres) and has important woodland, with oaks, hornbeam and beech. Horse riding, cycling and roller blading are encouraged. The Valley Gardens are perhaps the most beautiful natural area, but other places, including Virginia Water, are close rivals. The acidic soil of this part of Berkshire suits rhododendrons and azaleas, resulting in a spectacular display of flowers in spring.

Disabled parking and viewing platforms are provided. A whole book could be devoted to the attractions of Windsor Great Park and days could be spent exploring it on foot.

 HOW TO GET THERE

Windsor Home Park and Windsor Great Park [SU970770]

Windsor Castle is the obvious place to start. The Home Park is beside the B470, King Edward VII Avenue, close to the Riverside railway station. The Great Park extends for 5 miles south from Windsor Castle, beginning with formal gardens. There are car parks beside the main roads bordering the Great Park (A322, A329 and A30) and in the Home Park. Trains run from Waterloo and Paddington to two stations in Windsor. Moorings can be found in Windsor. The Valley Gardens and Virginia Water are open at all times.

www.theroyallandscape.co.uk

HOW TO GET THERE

Runnymede [SU997733]

Runnymede is beside the A308 between Windsor and Egham (near Staines). The National Trust car park is at the Windsor (northern) end [SU997733], and Runnymede Council has a car park at the Egham end [TQ007724]. The Thames Path runs through the reserve. Mooring is permitted beside the reserve (but charges are made, even for day visits). Egham Station is the closest. There is a bus service between Windsor and Egham. Runnymede is open at all times.

www.nationaltrust.org.uk/runnymede

95 Runnymede

The National Trust has a large expanse of riverside meadows and wooded hillside, in addition to the famous memorials. Most visitors will go to the Magna Carta memorial site. The Kennedy Memorial requires a climb among trees carpeted by wood anemones to a place where you can contemplate both the fine and the sad sides of human nature. The meadows are managed to encourage wildflowers and there are more adventurous walks.

For the more energetic, there is a steep climb through a wood above the Magna Carta memorial to reach the Air Force memorial high above the Thames Valley. For those who like to explore nature on the level, there is a 4 mile walk across the meadows to the long ponds and back to the river and the Thames Path, which makes a circular walk.

The tearoom near the National Trust car park has toilets available (when open). There are also toilets and a café at the council car park.

Long pond at Runnymede
– away from the main
visitor attractions

The magnificent trunk of the Ankerwyke yew tree

96

Ankerwyke Yew

The National Trust's Runnymede Estate has land on both sides of the river. It includes Magna Carta Island, although there is some uncertainty about exactly where King John signed the Magna Carta. On the Wraysbury side, the main attraction is an ancient yew tree, possibly as old as the Magna Carta. This is magnificent with a wonderful twisted trunk. Close to the yew tree are the remains of the priory that once covered this part of the National Trust land. The meadow nearest the car park has a fine example of hedging. The notice board advertises guided tours and volunteer activities; for more information, contact the National Trust at Runnymede (tel: 01784 432 891). It is open at all times, and dogs are permitted.

There are several circular walks on the National Trust land that go by the yew tree and along the Thames. There is a longer Wraysbury circular walk, which starts from the village and goes round Wraysbury gravel pits at the southern Colne Valley Park (see page 141).

Wraysbury village is the closest place to find a pub and other facilities (within a mile).

HOW TO GET THERE

Ankerwyke Yew [TQ005732]

Magna Carta Lane, Wraysbury. Magna Carta Lane is a small turning off the B376 between Wraysbury and Staines. From junction 13 on the M25, follow signs to Wraysbury. Look for Magna Carta Lane some 1½ miles after leaving the M25. The Thames Path runs on the opposite side of the river through Runnymede and does not have a convenient route to reach Ankerwyke. The same applies to the moorings at the National Trust land at Runnymede. If only there were a ferry! Wraysbury Station on the line between Staines and Windsor is probably the easiest way of arriving by public transport. There is a bus service (60 and 61) between Slough and Eton Wick that runs through Wraysbury.

www.wraysbury.net/history/magnacarta.htm

Ankerwyke yew tree ···· Hythe End ···· Wraysbury ···· Magna Carta Island ···· Ankerwyke yew tree

4½ MILES

This circular walk begins at Ankerwyke and goes in an anticlockwise direction. The similar walk in the reverse direction, and starting in Wraysbury, is described by the Colne Valley Park Partnership (www.colnevalleypark.org.uk). From the National Trust car park and information board in Magna Carta Lane, walk to Ankerwyke Yew and the remains of the priory. Continue towards the river, crossing a meadow to a stile. Take the path veering left beside the river, which does an S bend. The riverside path ends at a wall, where you turn left away from the river. After 50 yards you will see a metal gate in the wall with a sign about a private road. If the gate is open

Blackthorn arches over the path between a lake and houses in Wraysbury

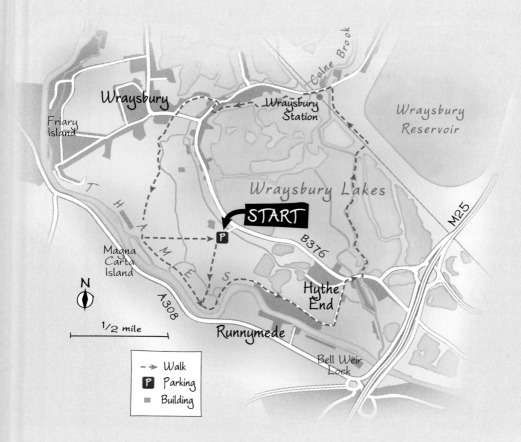

you can walk through to Hythe End Road and walk round until it meets the B376 in Hythe End village. Or you can stay on the footpath until it reaches the B376 opposite the Silver Wings Sailing Club, and turn right towards Staines (there is a pavement beside the road). At Hythe End, walk beside the B376 across the bridge over the Colne Brook. On the far side of the bridge, there is a footpath on your left, which enters Wraysbury Lakes. Here you'll find an information board about the lakes and conservation. The footpath runs between the Colne Brook for a third of a mile to the railway line. Cross carefully, and follow the path between the railway and the embankment of Wraysbury Reservoir. At the end of this path, it veers to the right to reach the road bridge over the Colne. Here turn left, past Wraysbury Station, and look for a track on your left into Tithe Barn. At the end of this cul-de-sac, there is a footpath that goes between a lake and a row of houses. This ends at a street with a church and windmill opposite. Turn right, and then first left, to walk behind the windmill and along the village green. When you meet a main road, turn right and look for a lane on your left to St Andrew's Church. Through the churchyard is a path crossing fields that leads you back to Magna Carta Lane. This lane leads to Magna Carta Island and is private property. If you turn left along the lane, you will go directly back to the car park. You can also stroll on through the field to return by the riverbank close to where the Magna Carta may have been signed.

River Colne by Wraysbury Lakes

97 Wraysbury Lakes

Wraysbury Lakes are former gravel pits now used for sailing, diving and fishing. The lake by Hythe End village is a nature reserve, but all the lakes attract water birds in winter when water sports are less active. Running among the lakes is the River Colne and a footpath from Wraysbury to Hythe End [TQ017727]. To visit the lake that is a nature reserve, park in Wraysbury or Hythe End and use the directions described in the circular walk on pages 140-141.

Did you know...
There are more than 190 islands in the Thames from Kent to Oxfordshire, and only 45 are inhabited by small settlements.

98 Truss's Island

The island commemorates Charles Truss who worked for the City of London when it managed the navigation of the Thames up to Staines. Appointed in 1774, Truss did much to improve the locks, banks and dredging of the Thames between London and Staines.

The island is an early example of conservation because it had been neglected in Truss's lifetime. In 1827, local volunteers planted it with shrubs, and these volunteers were the women in General Scott's family. The image of ladies in crinoline skirts planting bushes is very different from the modern conservation volunteers!

Now the island provides a popular feeding place for swans, geese and ducks. There is also a picnic area, with wooden sculptures where children can play. Fishing is permitted, with an area reserved for the disabled.

One of the sign boards describes the sacred nature of the Thames.

 HOW TO GET THERE

Truss's Island [TQ034699]

Chertsey Lane (A320), Thorpe. There is a car park and a bus stop beside the island. Mooring is permitted and is suitable for small boats. Larger boats can moor in Penton Hook Marina. There is also a public slipway to launch small boats. The Thames Path is on the opposite bank, but there is a path from Penton Hook Lock and Penton Hook Island to Temple Gardens and Chertsey Lane. Open at all times.

www.runnymede.gov.uk and search for 'Truss's Island'

Waterfowl at Truss's Island

99 Thorpe Hay Meadow

● HOW TO GET THERE

Thorpe Hay Meadow [TQ030702]

From Egham, take a path in Huntingfield Way, 200 yards southwest of Thorpe Lea School. Go southeast along the path for ¼ mile to reach the meadow. Another approach starts at Truss's Island car park (see Truss's Island, page 143). From the car park, cross the A320 main road to Green Lane, and go along Green Lane for a third of a mile to where a signed footpath crosses Green Lane (by now a track). Turn right to take this footpath around two sides of a lake. You will pass through a large area of brambles and muddy tracks, which is a former landfill site now used by quad bikes. In the southeast corner of this rough ground, a bridge crosses a stream to a metal gate. Pass through the gate to enter Thorpe Hay Meadow. The Thames Path is on the far side of the river and the closest point is at Staines Bridge. Penton Hook Marina is near Truss's Island. There are trains to Staines, and buses along the A320.

Thorpe Hay Meadow is a traditional hay meadow on Thames Gravel, rated as a Site of Special Scientific Interest (SSSI); some areas are sufficiently marshy for reeds. It is managed by Surrey Wildlife Trust, open at all times, and is used by those walking their dogs. It is not easy to find, and can only be reached by footpaths.

Thorpe Meadow

100

Penton Hook Island

Did you know...
The tidal range of
the Thames Estuary
at London Bridge is
up to 25 feet.

Penton Hook Island was created when a lock was cut across the neck of land around which the Thames flowed in a tight loop or 'hook'. The island is managed by the Environment Agency as a nature reserve, and it is reached by crossing the lock from the Thames Path.

The island has a good cover of shrubs and trees for birds, small mammals and insects. The Thames Angling Conservancy has built 'beetle lodges' – stacks of logs that shelter small creatures and will feed them as the wood rots. There is a strong fishing interest, with a stream running through the island that is ideal for fish spawning – you can look into the clear waters and see the fish. One of the weirs is built in steps, which makes it easier for migrating fish, particularly salmon, to get up the river to breed.

Watching the water pouring over the weirs you can see how air gets mixed in, enriching the oxygen content of the river. There are benches and signs commemorating the fishermen who loved this reserve. The paths around the island have good surfaces, but a wheelchair would have to be able to get onto the lock gates. Dogs should be kept on a lead.

HOW TO GET THERE

Penton Hook Island [TQ044696]

Penton Hook Lock, Laleham TW18. From the centre of Staines, take the Laleham Road, the B376. After three-quarters of a mile from the railway bridge, turn right into Wheatsheaf Road. Approaching the end of Wheatsheaf Road, turn left into Penton Avenue. Park at the end of the Avenue, and walk onto the Thames Path, and go left to the lock. The Thames Path downstream (east) from Penton Hook Lock can be reached by a path from River Way, another road off the B376. If visiting by boat, ask the lock-keeper for advice on where you can moor for the short time that you would need to visit the island. It is possible to moor in Penton Hook Marina and row across the weir stream to land on the island, provided that you do not interfere with fishing.

A 'beetle lodge' on
Penton Hook Island

101 Chertsey Meads

➜ HOW TO GET THERE

Chertsey Meads [TQ055662]

Mead Lane, Chertsey. There is good car parking space at the end of Mead Lane. The Thames Path is on the opposite side of the river, but there is a good path from Chertsey Bridge. Mooring is available at Chertsey Lock, and it is possible for small boats to moor on the banks of the meads. Open at all times.

www.surreycc.gov.uk/recreation-heritage-and-culture/tourism-in-surrey/visitor-attractions-and-accommodation/leisure-and-recreation/parks-and-gardens/chertsey-meads

Chertsey Meads is a large expanse of flood meadows that is full of flowers in summer. With Dumsey Meadow on the opposite bank of the river, the Meads provide public access to a substantial green area between Chertsey and Shepperton. There are many paths to explore, and the paths going to the riverside are suitable for wheelchairs. The tracks across the meadows on the south side, near the Bourne stream, can be very wet after heavy rain – so wear waterproof footwear if you are walking your dog here. The horse riding routes are signposted and have enough space to stop the ground from becoming muddy.

Most of the meadow flowers are common – dandelions in spring and clover in summer. They flourish because they are good sources of nectar for insects and get pollinated as a result. They make a cheerful sight in their profusion.

There is a play area by the car park, and picnic tables beside the river.

Near the play area, a footpath leads through Bates Wharf boatyard and the new apartments to Chertsey Bridge, where there is both a hotel and pub for refreshments.

Chertsey Meads

102 Dumsey Meadow

As written on the information board at Dumsey Meadow, meadows like this were to be found all along the Thames only a few decades ago. These were meadows that had never been ploughed nor spread with artificial fertilisers. Grazing kept the grass short, and wildflowers could flourish. Dumsey Meadow is not as wet as Chertsey Meads, so there are fewer marsh plants and reeds. The website in the 'How to get there' box lists the plants that can be found here. The pollarded willows and clumps of hawthorn bushes shelter birds and insects.

The seats, views of the river and boats, and the Kingfisher pub by Chertsey Bridge offer a rest to tired walkers along the Thames Path. The meadow is used for Chertsey Regatta in August.

 **HOW TO GET THERE**

Dumsey Meadow [TQ055667]

Chertsey Bridge Road, the B375. There is car parking (pay and display). The Thames Path goes along the river edge of the meadow. Mooring is available at Chertsey Lock, and it is also possible for small boats to moor on the banks of the meadow. Open at all times.

www.english-nature.
org.uk/citation/citation_
photo/1007206.pdf

Dumsey Meadow

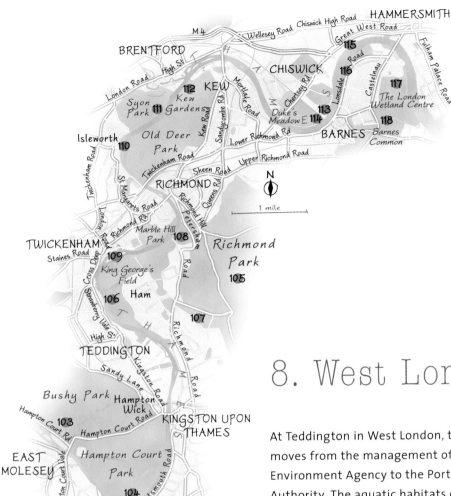

HAMMERSMITH

M4   Wellesey Road   Chiswick High Road

BRENTFORD   Great West Road   115

High St   CHISWICK   116

London Road   KEW   Mortlake Road   Chertsey Rd   Lonsdale Road   Castelnau   117   The London Wetland Centre

Syon Park   111   Kew Gardens   112   Sandycombe Rd   Kew Road   Duke's Meadow   113   118

Isleworth   Old Deer Park   110   Lower Richmond Rd   114   BARNES   Barnes Common

Twickenham Road   Twickenham Road   Sheen Road   Upper Richmond Road

St Margarets Road   RICHMOND   Queens Rd   N

London Road   Richmond Rd   Richmond Hill   Petersham Road   1 mile

TWICKENHAM   Marble Hill Park   108   Richmond Park

Staines Road   109   King George's Field   105

Cross Deep   106   Ham   107

Strawberry Vale   High St   Richmond Road   M

TEDDINGTON   Kingston Road

Sandy Lane   Bushy Park   Hampton Wick

Hampton Court Rd   103   Hampton Court Road   KINGSTON UPON THAMES

EAST MOLESEY   Hampton Court Vale   Hampton Court Park   104   Portsmouth Road   SURBITON

8. West London

At Teddington in West London, the Thames moves from the management of the Environment Agency to the Port of London Authority. The aquatic habitats change from fresh water to brackish and saltwater. The Royal Parks at Hampton Court and Richmond cater for a wide range of interests. The London Wetland Centre is a star attraction for birds. The reach between Teddington and Richmond is unique because the tidal gate at Richmond keeps the river level high and only allows the tide to flow up for two hours before high water. Once a year this reach is drained, exposing the riverbed. The foreshore at low tide is an important natural environment.

A quiet corner at
London Wetland Centre

103

Bushy Park

Bluebells in Bushy Park

▶ HOW TO GET THERE

Bushy Park [TQ160690]

Hampton Court Road, Hampton, Middlesex TW11 0EQ. The car parks are open from 6.30am to dusk. Open all the time, except September and November when open 8am to 10.30pm. Close to the Thames Path and cycle routes at Hampton Court Bridge. Public moorings at Hampton Court. Trains to Hampton Court, Hampton Wick and Twickenham Stations. Good bus services.

www.royalparks.org.uk/
parks/bushy_park

Bushy Park, with more than 1,000 acres, is the second largest of the Royal Parks. It is very different from the formal gardens in the grounds of Hampton Court Palace. Although linked to the Palace, it has a rural character, including the remains of a medieval farmland, a Tudor deer park, 17th-century water gardens and woodland.

The red and fallow deer roam freely in the park, as they did when Henry VIII used to hunt here. As the notices warn, the deer are wild creatures, but their body language suggests that they are a bit bored with being photographed. However, we could not resist! As seen in Bushy Park, deer have had a key effect on the landscape by shaping the trees. The lollipop shape, so typical in Constable paintings or children's drawings, is a result of the height that the deer can reach the leaves.

The woodland gardens are enclosed to protect the plants from deer. The gardens have introduced species – the brightest in spring are the rhododendrons and azaleas – but there are also plenty of native plants, from bluebells to birches. The woodlands are laced by streams and paths, and are a charming place to stroll around in peace. The peace is occasionally broken by the screeches of the ring-necked parakeets, a non-native species that have become the noisiest birds in west London and Surrey. In contrast are the lovely songs of warblers, thrushes and robins.

The visitor centre by the woodland gardens has a car park, café and information about the park, heritage trails, self-guided walks with maps, stopping points, images and audio guides.

The water gardens are based on the artificial Longford River that was created in 1638 by Charles I to bring water to Hampton Court Palace. The Longford River is fed by the River Colne, and is a wildlife habitat with water voles, freshwater mussels and fish. On page 141 the River Colne was mentioned as a feature of the Wraysbury circular walk. The link to the Longford river is a reminder that the wildlife habitats are often connected in several ways.

Fallow deer in Bushy Park

104

Hampton Court Home Park

▶ HOW TO GET THERE

Home Park [TQ160690]

Hampton Court Road,
Hampton, Middlesex TW11
0EQ. The car parks are
open from 6.30am to dusk.
Walk along Hampton Court
Road towards Kingston for
about 250 yards from the
main gate into Bushy Park,
to the Paddock entrance;
there is another entrance
at the Kingston Bridge end
of Hampton Court Road
[TQ174695] from the Thames
Path. There are moorings
at Hampton Court. There
are trains to Hampton
Court, Hampton Wick and
Twickenham stations, and
good bus services.

www.hrp.org.uk/
HamptonCourtPalace

Deer in Hampton Court Home Park

The Home Park at Hampton Court is a quiet place to escape the crowds in the palace and its gardens. The wilderness part of the park is the grassland on the north side of the Long Water (a golf course is on the south side). The straight avenues of trees may appear too formal for true wilderness, but they give splendid perspectives to the palace. There are other paths to wander around, looking at wildflowers or deer. You can get onto the banks of the Thames if you wish to walk back beside the river. The Home Park is open to the public throughout the year.

Hampton Court from the Home Park

105 Richmond Park

Richmond Park

Richmond is the largest of the Royal Parks in London, covering 2,500 acres. It has spectacular hill views over the Thames Valley and London to St Paul's Cathedral, 12 miles away. It is popular because it has good access by road and rail, lots of parking spaces, and well-marked paths, but it never feels crowded. Charles I made it into a deer park in 1637. He had the walls built to enclose it, thereby arousing local opposition that was appeased by permitting public access. The walls and public access have survived as symbols of compromise. In 1773, Charles II had new ponds dug, partly to make drinking places for deer, but also to extract gravel for building work in London after the Great Fire in 1666. The gravel industry in the Thames Valley has a long history!

The lowland acid grasslands of the Park are important in the UK Biodiversity Action Plan. This type of grassland, mixed with ancient woodland, has become uncommon in southern England. It is ideal for the herds of red and fallow deer that graze the grasses (49 species recorded) without compacting the soil. As long as the soil is kept low in nutrients, the wildflowers that are typical of acid grassland – harebells, heath bedstraw, bluebells – will flourish. The oak trees in the woods provide habitat for fungi and many species of beetles.

The Isabella Plantation was created after 1945 from existing woodland. Although it has non-native plants, the 100 species of azaleas and rhododendrons and 120 hybrids make a beautiful sight in spring. Richmond Park is a popular place for cycling on the designated tracks, horse riding, orienteering, jogging and cross country running.

Picnics are encouraged and a document to help plan picnics is available on the website. Volunteers help with staffing the visitor centre next to Pembroke Lodge – planting trees, clearing invasive rhododendrons, fund-raising and helping with educational programmes.

 HOW TO GET THERE

Richmond Park [TQ185735]

Richmond Park, Surrey TW10 5HS. Park gates are shut from dusk to 7.30am (7am in summer). To check, telephone 020 8948 3209. There are six free car parks. If coming by bus, take the 371 or 65 from Richmond Station to Petersham Gate. For trains and the Underground, it is Richmond Station. The Thames Path is close as it passes through Richmond. Richmond Park is on National Cycle Network Route 4 and the Capital Ring Walk. There are public moorings at Teddington Lock and Richmond.

www.richmond.gov.uk
www.royalparks.org.uk/
parks/richmond-park

Among the trees at Ham Lands

106

Ham Lands

HOW TO GET THERE

Ham Lands [TQ167720]

Riverside Drive, Richmond TW10 7UE. The nearest car park is at Ham House (National Trust). Ham Lands is beside the Thames Path, and close to National Cycle Network Route 4 (Teddington to Richmond). Mooring is available at Teddington Lock.

www.richmond.gov.uk
www.fohl.org.uk

This riverside nature reserve is an extensive area of grassland and scrub with abundant wildlife and a network of paths for excellent walking and wildlife observation on the outskirts of London. The land once had gravel pits that were refilled with soil and rubble from across London. This has created a mosaic of different vegetation types, attracting many species of butterflies and birds. There are small meadows with wildflowers surrounded by hawthorn bushes. On the western (river) side, there is a belt of trees, laced by paths that connect to the Thames Path on the riverbank. There is an active group of Friends of Ham Lands, who record the rarer plants and arrange community activity days.

107 Ham Common

Between Ham and Richmond Park is Ham Common, which has two parts. On the west of the A307 it is mown grassland and a small pond, with a village green atmosphere. The nature reserve is on the east of the A307 beside a road into Richmond Park [TQ185718]. When grazing stopped a century ago, it changed from grassland to oak and birch woodland, but there are still small meadows. It is an ideal place for dog walking, with a path away from roads along its southern perimeter. It is open at all times, so it might be suitable for listening to the dawn chorus on summer mornings before Richmond Park opens.

Did you know...
There are at least 125 species of fish and 350 species of bottom-dwelling invertebrates in the Thames.

Ham Common

108 Petersham Meadows

Petersham Meadows lie beside the river between Ham and Richmond [TQ181739]. They are open grassland, which was home to the last dairy herd in London. Cattle still graze on weekdays, but are put in a paddock at weekends because of problems with dogs. The view from the riverbank across the meadows to the Star and Garter Home on the hill has featured in paintings and photographs, and seems to have changed little in the past 100 years – a triumph of conservation. The meadows are used for walking and family recreation, and the hedges and trees give shelter to birds and insects.

The field poppy – a symbol of military courage

Petersham Meadows

Sand martin nests at Eel Pie Island

109 Eel Pie Island

The island was famous in the 1960s as a major jazz and blues venue. It is now occupied by private houses and boatyards that are reached by a footbridge from Twickenham.

The nature reserve is on the upstream (southwest) end of the island. There is an artificial sand cliff built for sand martins, which can be seen clearly from the Thames Path at TQ163729. A seat on the riverbank has a good view of the birds flying in and out of their nests. In the evening, you will also see bats. This can be watched via a webcam on www.thames-landscape-strategy. org.uk.

In winter when the sand martins are in Africa and the bats are hibernating, the seat is still a good place to watch the river, with black-headed gulls being the most noticeable birds.

 **HOW TO GET THERE**

Eel Pie Island [TQ163729]

The nature reserve on Eel Pie Island is best observed from the Thames Path in Ham at TQ163729. The reserve can only be visited by arrangement. The nearest car parking is at the National Trust property of Ham House.

www.thames-landscape-strategy.org.uk

110
Isleworth Ait

HOW TO GET THERE

Isleworth Ait [TQ167757]

Isleworth Ait lies mid-river opposite the mouth of the River Crane, and the famous London Apprentice pub. It can only be reached by boat by special arrangement, and is kept undisturbed as much as possible. It can be viewed from the Thames Path – better from the Richmond side, because the Path is diverted from the river edge in Isleworth. For this reason, Richmond Station is a better choice than Isleworth. Cycling is permitted along the riverbank.

www.wildlondon.org.uk and search for 'Isleworth Ait'.

Isleworth Ait is an island rated as a Site of Metropolitan Importance as a sanctuary for birds, beetles and two rare molluscs: the two-lipped door snail and German hairy snail. It has a tall canopy of mixed woodland, mostly poplar and willow. It was once an osier bed where the local willows were used to weave baskets to carry fruit and vegetables from Middlesex to the London markets.

The birds include treecreeper, kingfisher, heron, song thrush, goldeneye, house martin, grey wagtail, spotted flycatcher, dunlin, swallow and swift. Herons and cormorants perch on the branches over the water, while flocks of gulls (mostly black-headed) remind us that the main channel has the quaint name of Sheen Gulls.

Visits can be arranged by boat through the London Wildlife Trust and Greenspace Information for Greater London. A team of volunteers organised through the London Wildlife Trust have regular working parties.

Isleworth Ait

Syon Park

111 Syon Park

Syon House is the last surviving ducal residence in Greater London, home to the Duke of Northumberland. It is a 200 acre estate with parkland, 40 acres of garden, and an ornamental lake – a haven for wildlife, including terrapins.

The gardens, landscaped by Capability Brown in the 18th century, are famous for the 200 species of rare trees. It is a registered Grade I landscape in the English Heritage Register of Parks and Gardens of Importance in England.

Features include the London Tropical Zoo, a trout fishery, the Great Observatory, a garden centre, Maidenhead Aquatics, Buttercup Day Nursery, and the Snakes and Ladders indoor adventure playground.

HOW TO GET THERE

Syon Park [TQ175770]

Brentford, Middlesex, London TW7 6AZ. Car parking is included in the entry fee for the house and gardens. The Thames Path runs through Syon Park. If coming by bus it is the 237 and 267 to Brent Lea bus stop, or E2 or E8 to Brentford. If arriving by train, it is Kew Bridge (from Waterloo), and Underground to Boston Manor, Ealing Broadway or Gunnersbury and bus. Closed during the winter; open from March until October. Open hours are 11am to 5pm; entry fee charged.

www.syonpark.co.uk

112

Kew Royal Botanical Gardens

🢂 HOW TO GET THERE

Kew Royal Botanical Gardens [TQ190770]

Kew, Richmond, Surrey TW9 3AB. The South Circular Road (A205) passes the northeast corner of Kew Gardens, and Kew Road, the A307, runs on the east side. There are four entrances: Main, Victoria, Brentford and Lion Gates. The Thames Path passes the Brentford Gate. Cycle racks are provided at the entrances because cycles are not permitted in Kew Gardens. Kew Gardens Station is on the District Line and London Overground. Bus routes 65 and 391 stop near the main entrance. Public access is from 9.30am daily (except 24 and 25 December). Entry fee charged.

www.kew.org/visit-kew-gardens

Kew is famous for its 250 years of science and conservation work, as well as providing 300 acres of local park facilities, recreation, education and volunteering activities. There is also a wildlife observation area in the southwest corner.

Kew's botanic gardens are wonderful spaces; places to breathe fresh air and admire the beauty of nature. Kew's living collections includes 178,000 plants, with more than 19,300 species. The Herbarium houses around 7 million dried and pressed plant specimens and preserved collections. Four major attractions give ecological lessons while entertaining visitors:

- Princess of Wales Conservatory – ten climatic zones and a huge variety of plants.
- Temperate House – big glasshouse with the world's tallest indoor plant.
- Palm House – a tropical rainforest environment.
- Xstrata Treetop Walkway Lift – a tree canopy walkway.

Picnics and small group activities are encouraged in the open spaces.

The Old Deer Park on the western side of Kew Gardens has patches of wilderness beside the Thames Path and between the sports fields. These extend the green spaces along the river between Teddington Lock and Kew.

The Wilderness at Kew Gardens

113 Duke's Meadow

Much of Duke's Meadow is municipal parkland, with flowerbeds and mown grass. There are large sports fields around it, so it feels like a huge green space. A meadow is left uncut to encourage wildflowers, and shrubs and bushes provide nesting places and cover for small animals. There is a striking sculpture of a heron's nest and other wildlife images at the eastern end of the meadow. The riverbank is the biggest wildlife habitat, as it is covered with bushes and small trees, and the foreshore is a feeding ground for birds.

 HOW TO GET THERE

Duke's Meadow [TQ205765] and Duke's Hollow [TQ213763]

Riverside Drive, Chiswick W4 2SH, beside the A316. The Thames Path, on the north side of the Thames, runs through Duke's Meadow and past Duke's Hollow. The Thames Path is also a cycle path in this section. The nearest station is Barnes Bridge Station.

www.dukesmeadowstrust.org

114 Duke's Hollow

Duke's Hollow is a corner of London that has been allowed to 'go wild', with fallen trees, reeds and swampy patches. It is tucked in a corner between Barnes Bridge, Chiswick Rowing Club and Chiswick Rugby Ground. The entrance is marked by a wooden notice and is opposite to an entrance of the sportsground. There is a small viewing platform, but to see the reserve closely you will have to scramble down the bank, to get past the Japanese knotweed – a non-native invasive species.

Walking downstream from Duke's Hollow and Duke's Meadow on the same side will take you to Chiswick Eyot. If you cross Barnes Bridge, and go downstream (north), you will come to the Leg O'Mutton Nature Reserve.

The heron's nest sculpture at Duke's Meadow

115 Chiswick Eyot

HOW TO GET THERE

Chiswick Eyot [TQ219779]

Chiswick Mall, London W4 2PW. The Thames Path runs along Chiswick Mall, and this is part of a cycle route. Buses run along the A4. The nearest station is Stamford Brook Underground. There is open access at Chiswick Eyot when the tide permits, and Chiswick Pier has mooring for visiting boats.

Chiswick Eyot is smaller than Eel Pie Island and Isleworth Ait, but it is closer to the shore and easier to visit. At low tide there is a causeway of wet muddy stones from the Chiswick shore. The Eyot is covered by willows, scrubs and reeds. The nettles and dense vegetation are a sign of fertile soil, so it is no surprise that it was once used for growing fodder for horses and cattle. The narrow channel between the Eyot and the shore was used for trapping fish, including salmon, two centuries ago.

The Thames Explorer Trust, based at Chiswick Pier, organises walks along the foreshore. Volunteers with the organisation Thames21 help to clear litter and invasive plants from the Eyot (www.thames21.org.uk).

Flowering rush

Chiswick Eyot at low tide

Did you know...
Young eels migrate to the Thames from the Sargasso Sea, and stay for 20 years before going back across the Atlantic to spawn.

116

Leg O'Mutton Nature Reserve

Leg O'Mutton (Lonsdale) Nature Reserve is a former reservoir, saved from development by local action. It is a hidden treasure, not far from the famous London Wetland Centre, and its name of Leg O'Mutton describes its shape. In winter there are teal, tufted duck, widgeon and shovelers. The rafts floating on the lake are designed for waterfowl to nest, but turtles have adopted them to bask in the sun.

It is interesting to see how trees have colonised the brick and concrete sides of the reservoir and reeds have grown in shallow places. On a fine day, the Leg O'Mutton Reserve is a lovely place to sit and stare, before enjoying the nearby cafés and pubs in Barnes.

The British Trust for Conservation Volunteers helps to maintain the reserve.

HOW TO GET THERE

Leg O'Mutton Nature Reserve [TQ217772]

Lonsdale Road, Barnes SW13 9QN. When walking along the Thames Path between Barnes Bridge and Hammersmith Bridge on the south (Surrey) bank, look for a gateway in a wooden fence. You can follow a path beside the reservoir, and re-emerge onto the Thames Path at the other end, or continue round the lake. The Thames Path in this area is a cycle route. The nearest station is at Barnes Bridge. Street parking nearby is possible at weekends, and there is a car parking space in Lonsdale Road near the reserve. Open all the time.

www.richmond.gov.uk/
home/leisure_and_culture/
parks_and_open_spaces/
park_details.htm?parkId=200

The lake at Leg O'Mutton Nature Reserve

117 London Wetland Centre

⊙ HOW TO GET THERE

London Wetland Centre [TQ226767]

If driving, come via the A306 (Hammersmith to Barnes) to Queen Elizabeth's Walk, Barnes, London SW13 9WT. If you are taking the train, come from Waterloo, Clapham or Richmond to Barnes or Barnes Bridge. The Underground is to Hammersmith, and bus number 283. You can cycle or walk to the centre from the Thames Path to Queen Elizabeth's Walk. Open in daylight hours.

www.wwt.org.uk/london

In 1995 the Wildfowl and Wetlands Trust transformed the Barn Elms waterworks into a beautiful nature reserve, the London Wetland Centre. Its 100 acres are managed to provide water birds with wader scrapes, pools, lakes, meadows and gardens. More than 180 species of bird are seen each year and the centre is also home to other wildlife such as frogs, bats and dragonflies. Water voles and grass snakes have been released into the reserve and are now thriving. The centre has a collection of wildfowl from around the world, so visitors can look at the species arranged by the continent of origin. The most noticeable are the exotic blue winged geese and noisy white-faced whistling ducks.

For birdwatchers there are six hides dotted around the reserve. Every day there are different activities for those visiting the centre, and younger visitors will enjoy the two adventure play zones, plus a range of events at weekends and during school holidays. There is a café which provides meals and snacks, and a gift shop and binocular shop.

London Wetland Centre

118 Barnes Common

Barnes Common is a large (100 acres) area of common land which complements the London Wetland Centre. Like Richmond Park nearby, it is acid grassland on which gorse, broom and birch trees thrive. Parts of the common are sports fields, but the central part is still a wilderness. The paths weave between patches of gorse and under trees, and in the middle lies an old cemetery. In the northwest corner, the common becomes more formal with grass lawns around a pond. Beverley Brook runs along the north side of the common. This stream comes from Wimbledon and Merton, and can be followed by a path of the same name.

HOW TO GET THERE

Barnes Common [TQ223753]

Barnes Common lies to the north of the A305 (Richmond to Putney) and either side of the A306 (Hammersmith to Roehampton). There are no car parks for the common, but parking is possible in several places (e.g. the London Wetland Centre) and on the side streets at weekends. Barnes Station is near the centre of the common. The Thames Path is close by.

www.barnescommon.org.uk

Barnes Common

Parks and Gardens in London

In addition to the parks described in this and the next chapter, there are other parks and gardens in London that are green spaces near to the river and open to the public: Bishop's Park (Fulham), Wandsworth Park, Battersea Park, Ranelagh Gardens, the Royal Hospital at Chelsea, St James's Park and Southwark Park should be mentioned. Although not designated as nature reserves, they help to form a green corridor through London.

Hammersmith Bridge ···· London Wetland Centre ···· Barnes Common ···· Leg o'Mutton ···· Duke's Meadow ···· Chiswick Eyot ···· Hammersmith Bridge

8 MILES

From Hammersmith Bridge, take the Thames Path on the south (Barnes and Putney) side of the river, and walk southeast towards Putney. Look for the signs to the London Wetland Centre, on the right of the Thames Path. Assuming that you wish to visit the Wetland Centre (entry charge, but lots of good facilities), take this route. If walking via the Wetland Centre, the most direct way to Barnes Common is to turn left from Queen Elizabeth Walk to walk southwards until you see the common on the west side of the road. Look for a tarmac path that runs close to the northern edge of this part of the common, which will lead you to the northwest corner.

If you are not visiting the London Wetland Centre, you can continue along the Thames Path downstream until you see the sign for Beverley Brook Walk. Take this path to Barnes Common, crossing over the first concrete bridge that you see on your left. Crossing the common is a matter of following paths that lead in a westerly direction. If you have no compass and the sun is hidden, the flight path of aircraft to Heathrow will show you which way is west. If you are going in the right direction, you should pass by the old cemetery half hidden in the trees.

After exploring Barnes Common, find a path in the northwest corner of Barnes Green which crosses a small stream (Boundary Brook). Go to the right of a large pond to the A3003, Church Road. On the other side of Church Road, go along Nassau Road to reach the Thames and Lonsdale Road. Go right on Lonsdale Road until you find an entrance to the Leg O'Mutton Nature Reserve. Walk round the reservoir and leave the reserve at one of the gateways onto the Thames Path.

Take the Thames Path southwest (upstream) to Barnes Railway Bridge, which you cross.

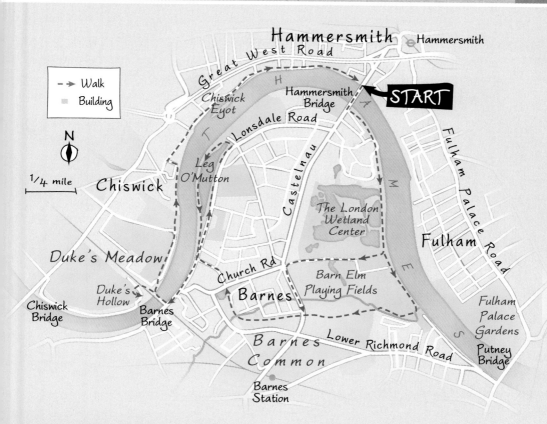

Hammersmith

Hammersmith

Great West Road

Walk

Building

N

1/4 mile

Chiswick Eyot

Hammersmith Bridge

START

Lonsdale Road

Leg O'Mutton

Chiswick

Castelnau

Fulham Palace Road

The London Wetland Center

Fulham

Duke's Meadow

Duke's Hollow

Church Rd

Barn Elm Playing Fields

Fulham Palace Gardens

Chiswick Bridge

Barnes Bridge

Barnes

Barnes Common

Lower Richmond Road

Putney Bridge

Barnes Station

On the north side of Barnes Bridge, the steps down are on the downstream side. Take the road leading away from the river and turn left under the railway embankment and back to the river to find Duke's Hollow on the upstream side. Having explored this corner of Duke's Meadow, return to the other side of the railway and follow the Thames Path towards Chiswick. As you walk beside the river in Duke's Meadow, look for wildlife in the bushes by the foreshore. Soon after leaving Duke's Meadow you will reach Chiswick Eyot. If you have timed your walk exactly right, you will be able to cross the channel to visit the Eyot. The walk finishes by following the Thames Path signs back to Hammersmith Bridge. This last section along Chiswick, Hammersmith and Lower Malls has good riverside pubs.

London Wetland Centre

9. East London

At first sight, the hard embankments of the Thames in central and east London may look inhospitable, but if you look more closely you will see plants and insects making their homes in the cracks. The foreshore can be considered as a linear nature reserve, with a rich variety of marine life and birds. Look down at low tide to see gulls feeding. Look up and you may be lucky enough to see a peregrine falcon, using the high buildings as cliffs. You can get down to the foreshore by the many steps and stairs, but be cautious: the mud and a rising tide can easily catch you unawares. The restoration of the docklands has re-created wildlife habitats: Bow Creek, East India Dock, Greenwich Peninsula Ecology Park, Lavender Pond, Russia Dock Woodland and Surrey Docks Farm show how well it can be done. Most of the other enclosed docks have enough water to accommodate resident populations of birds and fish; in time, they will be colonised by plants.

The Green Dock at the
Thames Barrier Park

119 Surrey Docks Farm

 HOW TO GET THERE

Surrey Docks Farm
[TQ365800]

South Wharf, Rotherhithe
Street, London SE16 5ET.
There is a car park near the
main gate at Rotherhithe. The
Thames Path and National
Cycle Network Route 4 pass
the farm. For those coming
by train, it is Surrey Quays
and Rotherhithe (London
Overground) and Canada
Water (Jubilee Line and
London Overground). By
bus it is the 381 Waterloo to
Peckham, and C10 Victoria
to Canada Water. If coming
via the river, Greenland Pier
is nearby. It is open daily
(except Mondays) from 10am
to 4pm (winter hours).

www.surreydocksfarm.org.uk

When you are walking or cycling along the Thames Path in east London, you will pass in front, behind and through blocks of flats. Suddenly in Rotherhithe, you will find that you are going through a farmyard instead of housing: the Surrey Docks Farm. As farms go, it is very small – 2 acres – but it is a working farm and is as close to the Thames as a farm can get, without being a fish farm. The attention is very much on animal welfare, with as much freedom of movement as possible in the available space. It provides experience of farming and horticulture. There are goats, cows, pigs, donkeys, sheep, poultry and vegetable plots; and herbs are grown in a formal garden by the entrance. The central farmyard has a herd of goats, and the orchard near the Rotherhithe Street entrance has beehives.

There is a small wildlife area, kept protected from the farm animals, at the southeast corner of the farm. In this area, there is a pond, piles of rotting wood, grasses and bushes. In a space the size of an urban garden, there are young birch, beech, cherry, hawthorn, apple and oak trees, with bluebells and primroses.

Education is a major function of Surrey Docks Farm. Activities include apple tasting, milking goats, butter making, vegetable growing, composting, pottery and a blacksmith's forge. Volunteers help with the animals, vegetables, building maintenance and the teaching.

*The wildlife garden pond
at Surrey Docks Farm – a
haven for frogs and insects*

120

Lavender Pond
Nature Park

Lavender Pond, just round the corner from Surrey Docks Farm, is a Local Nature Reserve based on part of the Surrey Docks. Originally the shallow pond was used for holding imported timber to stop it drying out. Then it became part of the reservoir that was used to maintain water levels in the Surrey Docks. The building of the pumping station used for this is now a museum and teaching centre next to the pond. In 1981, the pond was turned into a nature reserve, allowing reeds to grow and small islets to form, re-creating the riverside conditions before the docks were built 200 years ago. Sit on a bench here under the shade of a tree, looking at ducks on the water, and let your mind wander across the centuries of local history.

Lavender Pond is managed by the Trust for Urban Ecology (TRUE), who also manage Greenwich Peninsula Ecology Park and Stave Hill; TRUE have volunteers who help with the management.

 HOW TO GET THERE

Lavender Pond Nature Park [TQ363804]

Lavender Pond, corner of Lavender and Rotherhithe Roads SE16 5DZ. The Thames Path and National Cycle Network Route 4 pass the Surrey Docks Farm. For those coming by train, it is Surrey Quays and Rotherhithe (London Overground) and Canada Water (Jubilee Line and London Overground). By bus it is the 381 Waterloo to Peckham, and C10 Victoria to Canada Water.

www.urbanecology.org.uk/lavenderpark1.html

Did you know...
The first underwater tunnel was built in 1843 and now houses the East London rail line.

Lavender Pond

On Stave Hill

 HOW TO GET THERE

**Russia Dock Woodland
and Stave Hill Ecology Park
[TQ362798]**

There are entrances to the
Ecology Park at Redriff
Road, Downtown Road, and
Salter Road SE16. There is
parking for cars and bikes at
the Redriff Road entrance,
Downtown Road. If coming
by train, it is Canada Water
(Jubilee Line and London
Overground). If arriving by
bus it is the 381 or C10 along
Salter Road.

www.southwark.gov.
uk/info/461/a_to_z_of_
parks/664/russia_dock_
woodland/1

121

Russia Dock Woodland and Stave Hill Ecology Park

Following the closure of the Rotherhithe docks in the 1960s, the
Rotherhithe Peninsula was redeveloped. Russia Dock, once used
for importing timber from the Baltic, was a long body of water in
the centre of the peninsula. Now it is filled in and planted with
grass and trees to make recreational areas, and water channels
and ponds were made into habitats for kingfishers and herons.
The park has surviving dock features, including wall capstones
and mooring chains.

Stave Hill was built in 1985, using waste material and rubble.
A bronze model of the former docks stands at the top of the hill.
It is worth climbing the hill to get an understanding of what the
docks were like 50 years ago, and to look over east London to pick
out the various landmarks.

122 Mudchute Park and Farm

This farm of 32 acres is in the middle of the Isle of Dogs and has excellent views across to Canary Wharf. Next to the playing fields of Mudchute and Millwall Park, it was created in 1977 to preserve the green open space and protect the local environment. The mounds were made from the mud dredged from Millwall Docks. It provides a community facility for recreation, and a venue for seasonal events and private functions. The farm has more than 200 animals and fowl, and the East London Riding School and Equestrian Centre has stabling for 25 ponies and horses.

The Education Centre provides structured activities and courses in environmental education, science and farming topics linked to the National Curriculum. The centre has a nature trail, living classroom, children's nursery, and both after-school and youth clubs.

The farm has corporate volunteer days, and voluntary activities organised through the Orange RockCorps Project. Like other farms run on traditional lines, Mudchute has mud, animal droppings, spilt feedstuff, hedges, ponds and grazing land to support wildlife.

 HOW TO GET THERE

Mudchute Farm [TQ385787]

Pier Street, Isle of Dogs, London E14 3HP (tel: 020 7515 5901). There is a car park at Pier Street. The Thames Path and cycle route are close. If coming by train, it is the DLR Island Gardens and Mudchute Stations. Buses go to Pier Street. If coming via the river, it is Masthouse Terrace Pier. Mudchute Farm is open from Tuesday to Sunday, 9am to 4pm.

www.mudchute.org

Mudchute Farm

123

Bow Creek Ecology Park

HOW TO GET THERE

Bow Creek [TQ392812]

Silvertown Way, London E16 4ST. The entrance is on a path between Canning Town Station and Silvertown Way, where a footbridge crosses the Lea. The Thames Path and National Cycle Network Route CS3 are about a quarter of a mile away. If coming by train it is the DLR East India Station. There is a bus station near the Lea Mouth roundabout. Opening times are 8.30am to dusk.

www.leevalleypark.org.uk

Bow Creek is the tidal estuary of the River Lea and meanders for much of its 2 mile course to enter the Thames east of Canary Wharf. The banks of the Creek used to have gas works and derelict docks, but have benefited from the restoration of the lower Lea Valley. The Bow Creek Ecology Park is a narrow strip of land about 6 acres in size on a peninsula formed by a bend in the Creek. The Docklands Light Railway (DLR) crosses it, and gives shelter to an attractive teaching space. In contrast to the urban setting, reeds grow on the bank of the Creek and the grass areas are hay meadows. The management of riverside habitats is explained well in the demonstrations beside the path that runs the length of the reserve. The mudflats in the Creek attract teal and redshanks at low tide.

Bow Creek is part of the developments along the River Lea to link the Lea Valley Regional Park and Olympic Park to the Thames and to increase facilities and open spaces for the community. The Ecology Park was opened to the public in 2006.

Teaching space at Bow Creek

Did you know...
London's first solar-powered railway station has been built at Blackfriars and provides 50% of its own electricity.

124 East India Dock Basin

The East India Docks Reserve is the last remaining section of the docks where spices were imported from the Far East, and this history is reflected in the street names nearby. The dock is kept full of water, so it forms a lake. Shallows on the inner side have allowed a reedbed to grow under the shadow of the Lower Lea Crossing. There are seats and some grass, but most of the interest is in the lake and reeds. Interesting information boards tell the history of the docks. Instead of bird hides, metal screens help birdwatchers, and are in keeping with the industrial heritage. It is at the lower end of the Lea Valley, very close to Bow Creek Ecology Park. The Lea Valley is a migration route for birds, so these two reserves in the Lea Valley and the Greenwich Peninsula Ecology Park are important links in the chain of habitats through east London.

There is a ferry from Trinity Buoy Wharf, Orchard Place, to the O2 Pier in Greenwich. There is also a cable car service across the river, so that you can follow the birds.

HOW TO GET THERE

East India Dock Basin [TQ391808]

East India Dock is at Orchard Place, London E14 9QS. There are three entrances: in Orchard Place, from the Thames Path and Virginia Quay river frontage, and in the northwest entrance near the Lea Mouth roundabout. The closest car park is at the Excel Centre, a mile away. The Thames Path and National Cycle Network Route CS3 go past the Dock Basin. If coming by train, it is the DLR East India Station. There is a bus station near the Lea Mouth roundabout.

www.leevalleypark.org.uk
www.myleariverpark.org

East India Dock Basin

The Creekside Discovery Centre, Deptford

125

The Creekside Discovery Centre, Deptford

 HOW TO GET THERE

Creekside Discovery Centre, Deptford [TQ375773]

Creekside Centre, 14 Creekside, Deptford SE8 4SA. From Greenwich Station, exit along Tarves Way to Norman Road. Turn left, under the railway, to a path on the right side, by a signpost to Ha'penny Hatch Bridge. Across the bridge, you reach Creekside. The Thames Path crosses Deptford Creek on the A200, and Norman Road is on the east side; a cycle route runs with the Thames Path. If coming by bus, it is routes 47, 53, 177, 188, 199 or 453. If coming via the river, it is Greenwich Pier.

www.creeksidecentre.org.uk

Creek is the mouth of the River Ravensbourne and was formerly a busy tidal dock, but only one wharf is still working. At low tide the muddy basin attracts waders and gulls to feed, and the Creekside Discovery Centre arranges walks at low tide to look for shellfish and plants. The creek can only be visited at low tide, and by arrangement. Volunteers are welcome, to help with clean-ups and running the Discovery Centre.

126 Greenwich Park

Greenwich Park has a spectacular position overlooking the Thames. The park's important wildlife features are the trees, gravel heathland on One Tree and Crooms Hills, and the Wilderness. The Wilderness is an enclosed area, with red and fallow deer, near Blackheath Gate. There are waterfowl on the pond and warblers, woodpeckers, treecreepers and tawny owls in the trees. Specialised invertebrates in the park include the oak bush-cricket, 92 species of spider, and 14 butterfly species.

The avenues of sweet chestnut trees are 400 years old and are home for pipistrelle bats. An old orchard is being restored into a community garden and education area, and extends the wildlife friendliness of the park. The Secret Garden Wildlife Centre has information about the flora and fauna of the park.

Friends of Greenwich Park arrange activities for volunteers to monitor species and restore habitats.

Other things to see are the Observatory, the National Maritime Museum and the Cutty Sark.

The view from Greenwich Park

HOW TO GET THERE

Greenwich Park [TQ390774]

Blackheath Gate, Charlton Way, Greenwich SE10 8QY. You can park at weekends and bank holidays at Blackheath Gate. The Thames Path and National Cycle Network Route 4 are close by. If coming by train, it is the DLR Cutty Sark Station and Maze Hill (National Rail). If coming by bus, it is route 188 to Greenwich Park Gate. If arriving via the river, it is Greenwich Pier. Greenwich Park is open from 6am for pedestrians and 7am for traffic, all year round.

www.royalparks.org.uk/ parks/greenwich-park

Tower Bridge ···· Isle of Dogs ···· Greenwich ···· Rotherhithe ···· Tower Bridge

12 MILES

Designing a circular walk to explore wilderness habitats in the middle of east London is a challenge. The Thames Path is an obvious foundation, but it uses streets where the riverside is blocked by buildings. Tower Bridge and the Greenwich foot tunnel are the only ways in east London to cross the Thames on foot. By boat, the distance from Tower Bridge to Greenwich is 4 miles, but the twists and turns of the Thames Path on both sides of the river stretch the Thames Path distance to about 6 miles on each side. Add more for rambling around reserves or climbing the hill in Greenwich Park, and you will find (and feel!) that you have walked well over 12 miles by the time you get back to your starting point. Using public transport, or reducing the size of the circle by the ferry from Canary Wharf to Hilton Hotel Pier, Rotherhithe, is a shorter walk. Much of the route can be cycled, but you would have to walk for some of the way (eg through the Greenwich foot tunnel). A warning – this is not a walk for people who hate tunnels.

The walk is likely to take four to six hours: for some of the time, the tide will be low and the foreshore exposed. This will add to the interest of the riverside sections where you can get down to the foreshore.

Starting on the north bank at Tower Bridge, use the Thames Path in front of the large hotel to go across the lock entrance of St

Canary Wharf

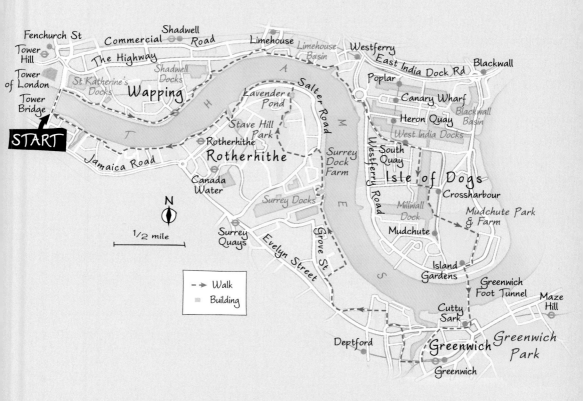

Katharine's Dock and around the Dickens Inn to St Katharine's Way. At the end of St Katharine's Way, the route is along Wapping High Street, past the Hermitage Memorial Gardens. These gardens are the first of many small urban parks on the route that are reminders of a greener environment. The Thames Path weaves repeatedly to the riverfront and back behind buildings. Some riverfront sections are closed at night, so you have to keep looking for the signs and testing whether gates are locked or just appear to be closed. If the tide is low, you may like to go down to one of the steps in Wapping to explore the foreshore.

After 3 miles of navigating the Thames Path, you leave it at West Ferry Circus. Go towards Heron Quay and Marsh Wall and follow Marsh Wall round to South Quay. As you pass the docks, look out for water birds – coots, grebes, tufted duck and mallards – that have made their homes in the financial centre. More could be done to give them some natural cover – for example, on rafts planted with reeds. The grebes and cormorants are a healthy sign that there are plenty of fish. After walking under the DLR bridge across Marsh Wall, turn right to walk beside Millwall Inner Dock. Cross to the east side by the lifting bridge, and go further down to the inner end of the Millwall Outer Dock, where there is a raised semi-circular platform. Beside the platform, take the path signposted to East Ferry Road. Emerging from a tunnel under the DLR, you will see a path sloping up to Mudchute Park on the other side of the road. Here is a large green space and the first reserve on the walk. At 4 miles, there will be some sighs of 'At last!' It is lovely to have grass and mud underfoot as you walk across the park and through the farm. Loos, views and booze are essential ingredients in the tourist business. If you count tea as booze, Mudchute Farm provides all three. If not, wait until you get to Greenwich. When ready to move on, leave the farm by its main entrance and turn right through a narrow passage signposted to DLR Island Gardens. Go straight down Stenbondale Street by Millwall Park, turn right in Manchester Road, and cross over opposite the DLR station to go along Douglas Path into Island Gardens and the entrance to the Greenwich Foot Tunnel.

On the far side of the river, the sense of being in a confined space will be instantly relieved as you come out by the Cutty Sark and her soaring masts. There are plenty of pubs around you; the National Maritime Museum and the park provide the other tourist essentials. This is about halfway round the walk, and only you can decide how much you wish to look round Greenwich before continuing the circular walk.

The route back starts with the Thames Path again, along Horseferry Place and Norway Street. If you are interested in finding the Creekside Discovery Centre from Norway Street, cross the busy Creek Road (A200) to Norman Road. When you have passed under a railway bridge, turn right along a path marked as a cycle route. This path crosses Deptford Creek and gets to Creekside next to the Centre. You can see what goes on in the Centre by looking through gaps in the wall, but you are advised to find out when the Centre is open before making a diversion to it. From the Centre, go north (under the railway) along Creekside, passing another small city park (Ferranti Park), back to the main road. Crossing the main road to go down the short Gonson Street brings you to the Stowage. You are back to the route of the Thames Path after a diversion of about half a mile.

In the Stowage, turn left to find the Thames Path signs, pointing past St Nicholas Church into McMillan Street. In McMillan Street, the Path turns right though another park to Princes Street. At the end of Princes Street, follow the Thames Path signs through Sayes Court Park to get to Grove Street. Walking northwards along Grove Street brings you to Pepys Park. Turn right into the park, follow the path between blocks of flats, up some steps, and into the upper part of Pepys Park. Part of this area is being turned into a wildlife habitat, with bushes and rough grass. The seats and picnic tables make this a good place to rest, with a view over the river embankment. From here to Surrey Docks Farm, the Thames Path runs along the riverfront (Deptford Strand) for most of the way, except for a short inland section along Odessa Street.

From Surrey Docks Farm (another place with a café and seats), go into Rotherhithe

Pepys Park - a green space amidst blocks of flats

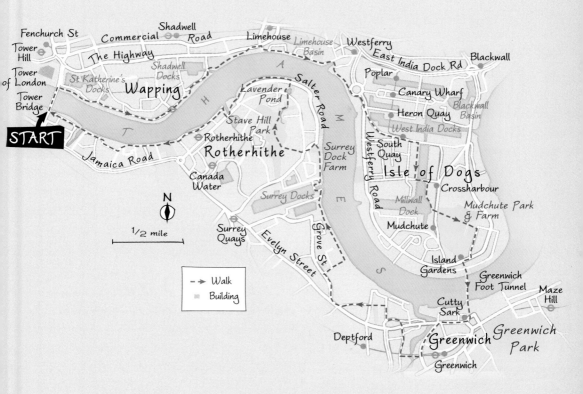

Street which curves westward to a junction with Salter Road. Cross Salter Road, then turn right for a short distance to go into Downtown Road which leads into an entrance to the Russia Dock Woodland. Ahead is a path to Stave Hill and its Ecological Park. There is such a network of paths in the Ecological Park that it is hard to describe a route through it. If you get to its northeast corner, you will find a path beside a duck pond. This path goes to the entrance in Downtown Road in one direction; in the other direction it curves through the northern end of Russia Dock to reach Salter Road near Bywater Place and Lavender Pond Reserve.

From Lavender Pond, it is a short distance to cross Rotherhithe Street and reach the Thames Path where it takes a riverside way along Sovereign Crescent. The route is now on the Thames Path for the rest of the walk. Like the northern banks, there is a mixture of riverside walks and streets behind buildings. You will cross Kings Stairs Gardens which are the northern end of Southwark Park – more urban green space. At last, Tower Bridge comes into sight. When you come to the end of Bermondsey Wall (a street behind riverside buildings), look carefully for a sign to St Saviour's Dock. It is worth pausing to look for ducks and other wildlife as you cross the pretty bridge at the dock. There is a final stretch of riverside and a street (Shad Thames), and you go up the steps onto Tower Bridge to complete the circle. On the Bridge and around the Tower, the thrust of the crowds of visitors may make you appreciate the wilder, quieter passages of the walk.

127 Greenwich Peninsula Ecology Park

◉ HOW TO GET THERE

Greenwich Peninsula Ecology Park [TQ392795]

John Harrison Way, Greenwich SE10 0QZ. The reserve is between the Greenwich Millennium Village and the river. The entrance is on the Thames Path, which is also a cycle path. If coming by train, it is the North Greenwich (Jubilee Line) and Charlton (National Rail). There are good local bus services – the nearest stop is Millennium Village Oval Square. If coming via the river, it is the O2 Pier. Greenwich Yacht Club and its moorings are next to the reserve. The outer lake area is open all the time. The inner lake area is reached by a gatehouse which is open from 10am to 5pm (except Mondays and Tuesdays).

www.urbanecology.org.uk/gpep.html

The park is a freshwater habitat with inner and outer lakes, home to frogs, newts, toads, dragonflies, damselflies and birds. The original marshes were destroyed by the excavation of the Blackwall Tunnel in 1897 and by subsequent industry. The land became derelict until regeneration started in 1970 when 300 acres of land were brought back to life.

In spring and summer, the wildflower meadow becomes alive with butterflies, moths (200 species recorded), 38 bee species (three rare) and nine types of wasps. At a recent Dawn Chorus event, 37 bird species were heard in the park. The park has a network of wooden boardwalks suitable for wheelchairs. The boardwalk around three sides of the inner lake takes you to two bird hides.

Volunteer activities take place two days a week. They include reedbed maintenance, species monitoring, building bat boxes, weeding, and tree care. There are weekend workshops and organised activities, including evening bat walks, spider art classes, pond dipping and family fun days. A primary school activity programme covers a range of subjects – from science through art to citizenship.

On the river edge, reedbeds have been planted from the O2 centre to the Ecology Park to restore the natural habitat and protect the bank against erosion.

Inner lake at Greenwich Peninsula Ecology Park

128

Thames Barrier Park

The Thames Barrier Park was opened on the north banks of the Thames in November 2000, following the regeneration of an industrial site in Silvertown by the London Development Agency. It now provides riverside community facilities for Newham residents and visitors to southeast London. Its features are fountains, family areas, flower gardens, wildflower meadows, a children's play area, a five-a-side football/basketball court, and lawns overlooking the Thames Barrier.

The park is wheelchair friendly, and is a welcome green oasis amid the stark concrete of modern development in Silvertown. Most striking are the contoured yew hedges that represent a Green Dock. The wide range of shrubs and flowers reflect the ever-changing spectrum of river tones. The straight lines of tree planting and rectangular designs may not appear wild, but maturity will bring more nesting places to add to the boxes in the trees by the café.

 HOW TO GET THERE

Thames Barrier Park [TQ415793]

North Woolwich Road, London E16 2HP. There is car parking in the Thames Barrier Park. If coming by train, it is the DLR Pontoon Dock. If arriving by bus, it is route 474. The Thames Path is on the opposite (south) side of the river, but there is a good cycle track under the DLR from Canning Town. It is open daily from 7am to dusk.

www.gardenvisit.com/ garden/thames_barrier_park

Young birch trees at Thames Barrier

Yellow flag

129 Crossness Nature Reserve

Crossness Nature Reserve was created in 1996, as a small oasis within an industrial urban environment. It is one of the last remaining areas of grazing marshes in London, and was part of the extensive Erith Marshes linked to the reserves in the next chapter of this book (Crayford and Dartford Marshes). The open access site is an area of 50 acres of reedbeds, ditches, pools, mudflats, scrub and rough grassland. More than 130 species of bird have been recorded here, including squacco heron, purple heron and quail.

HOW TO GET THERE

Crossness Nature Reserve [TQ492793]

The Old Works, Crossness S.T.W., Belvedere Road, Abbey Wood, London SE2 9AQ. There is access from the cycle paths and footpaths that run along the south shore of the Thames, from Eastern Way on the A2016, Norman Road, and Belvedere Road. No parking is available at the nature reserve, but there is a car park for the Crossness Engines. The Thames Path and National Cycle Network Route 1 pass the reserve. If coming by train, Abbey Wood and Belvedere Stations are the closest. If arriving by bus, it is Norman Road, routes 180, 401, 601.

www.crossness.org.uk
www.wildlifeextra.com/go/uk/reserve-crossness

Crossness Nature Reserve

There are nesting boxes for barn owls, a wader scrape, a bat cave, a shingle island and a sand martin wall. Water voles live in the new wetlands and invertebrates thrive in the reedbeds.

The reserve attracts good numbers of wintering wildfowl including teal, widgeon, gadwall and shoveler. The wet meadow is a high tide roost for lapwing, redshanks and dunlin. Important flora species are also found here, including knotted-hedge parsley, Borrer's saltmarsh grass and marsh dock.

As well as looking for wildlife in the Crossness Nature Reserve, it is worth walking along the Thames Path in front of the water treatment buildings. There are viewing places that look onto the river and mudflats at Halfway Reach Bay, where birds will come to feed as the tide ebbs. The outfall of water from the treatment works attracts gulls, always on the scrounge for a meal.

The industrial history of the area is well described on information boards along the Thames Path. If you can, do visit the steam-powered Crossness Engines in the Victorian pumping station, built by Sir Joseph Bazalgette for the London sewage system.

Did you know...
The rare short-snouted seahorse was recorded in the Thames at Greenwich during a fish survey in 2012.

10. North Kent

As you explore from the Thames Barrier to the sea, the tidal mudflats and saltmarshes become the dominant habitats, where bird reserves such as the Elmley Marshes have become justly famous. The South Saxon Shore Way takes over from the Thames Path to continue the long-distance path along the north Kent coast. In places it becomes lonely and difficult to find links to public transport, but walking is the best way to learn about the wilderness places along the coast.

Swale Nature Reserve

130 Crayford Marshes

Demoiselle

Crayford Marshes

Crayford Marshes is an area of grazing land that has been saved from development because of the risk of flooding. It is a reserve managed by the RSPB. The path from Slade Green and beside the River Darent makes a pleasant walk down to the Thames and Crayford Ness. The path passes Howbury Farm, which was a moated farmstead (hence the name of the lane from Slade Green). The farmstead dates from the 9th century and features a tithe barn that is 400 years old. From Moat Lane the path has a firm surface as it passes between blackthorn and hawthorn bushes until it reaches the seawall by the Darent. On the other side of the Darent, towards Queen Elizabeth Bridge, lie Dartford Marshes, which can also be visited by following the Saxon Shore Way and cycle path around via Crayford.

There is a good 4 mile circular walk starting at the seawall. Turn left (north) and go along the seawall, until you come to the tall structure of the flood barrier. From here you can view the mudflats which attract waders and wildfowl, and the seawall path goes west to Crayford Ness. Looking across the Thames you will see the impressive RSPB centre at Rainham Marshes.

From Crayford Ness you can retrace your steps or go on to make a circular walk back to Slade Green. If going on, you pass Erith Yacht Club, and take the signposted cycle path that leads to Slade Green Road. This will bring you to Forest Road and the rail station.

The marshland birds observed here include black-tailed godwit, snipe, teal, dunlin, shellduck, little grebe, redshank, oystercatcher, lapwing, heron and kingfishers. Water voles are also present.

HOW TO GET THERE

Crayford Marshes [TQ533770]

Crayford Marshes, Bexley DA8 2LA. From the A206 in Erith, go to Slade Green Station. From the station in Forest Road, go down Moat Lane to the marshes. The track continues to Crayford Ness on the Thames. There is street parking near Slade Green Station. National Cycle Network Route 1 and the Saxon Shore Way run round the reserve, and provide another way of reaching the reserve from Crayford. If coming by bus, it is the 89, 469 and 428. If coming by boat, moorings can be arranged at Erith Yacht Club.

www.bexleyrspb.org.uk/reserves/crayford-marshes.php

Did you know...
Seals breed and nurse their young in the Thames Estuary and have been recorded as far upstream as Waterloo Bridge.

131 Dartford Marshes

HOW TO GET THERE

Dartford Marshes [TQ543771]

If you are coming by car, drive from Dartford town centre, and head towards Erith until you reach a large roundabout. Turn right here, along Bob Dunn Way (the A206) towards the M25. After crossing Dartford Creek, turn left at the next roundabout and go left. Drive along this narrow road, Joyce Green Lane, down onto the marsh. Park at the point at which it is not possible to go any further and walk to the Thames riverfront. The marshes are near National Cycle Network Route 1. If you are coming by train, walk from Dartford Station, and follow the signs for the Darent Valley Path which will take you by the river to the marshes.

Dartford Marshes are a fragment of marshland that once stretched all the way along the Thames Estuary. What remains is a collection of arable fields, grazing land, motorcycle trails and scrubland criss-crossed by drainage ditches. The conservation is managed by Dartford Borough Council. One reason why the land was saved from development in the 20th century was because of the Joyce Green Hospital, which was built as an isolation hospital, to replace the hospital ships in Long Reach that had been used as quarantine stations for sailors. It was used for treating smallpox, diphtheria and scarlet fever. It had horse-drawn trams to take patients to and from the pier at Long Reach. The Joyce Green Hospital was eventually closed and demolished in 2000. Dartford Creek (River Darent) meets the River Thames at a barrier that controls tidal flows.

Given the somewhat degraded habitat, a surprising number of birds come in the spring and autumn migratory periods, and stay to over-winter here. The breeding birds are mainly common species, but black redstarts and a peregrine falcon have bred at Littlebrook Power Station.

The mudflats exposed at low tide at the mouth of Dartford Creek and nearby sewage outfalls attract birds to feed. Gulls are present all year round, and also yellow-legged gulls (recently identified as a separate species, but similar to herring gulls).

There is a small gravel pit turned into a lake beside Bob Dunn Way, which is worth a look if going eastward along the A206 (pull off into a gateway with a footpath sign, after crossing the bridge over the creek, TQ538771). When visited in March 2012, there were more birds here than on the rest of the marshes. The footpath goes all the way down to the Thames, and might be a better way to visit the marshes than going along Joyce Green Lane. Water voles, marsh and common frogs inhabit the drainage ditches. Crayford Marshes and Littlebrook Reserves are close by.

Heron on Dartford Marshes

132 Littlebrook Nature Park

There is a small nature reserve with three lakes in the industrial development called Littlebrook Park, managed by Dartford Council. It is in the corner formed by the A206 junction with the M25. Surrounding the lakes are grassland and scrub. While none of the wildlife reported on the reserve are unusual species, it is a pleasant place to walk on a sunny day and the paths are suitable for wheelchairs. There is a striking statue of a mermaid, against the backdrop of Littlebrook Power Station.

The houses behind the industrial development are close to the site of the Joyce Green Hospital. The site was initially surveyed for its conservation value in 2000 and 2001. The survey found that the land was sandy heath, which was once common along the Thames Estuary, but is now relatively rare. Therefore the commitment in 2005 to conserve Littlebrook Nature Park was very welcome.

Sculpture at Littlebrook Nature Park

HOW TO GET THERE

Littlebrook Nature Park [TQ552758]

The Bridge, Dartford. From Junction 1A on the M25, take the A206 to Erith. At the first roundabout, half a mile from the M25, take the second exit into The Bridge site (a business and residential park). There is no official public car park, so permission should be sought. Open access by footpaths and cycle tracks. Dartford Station is about 1½ miles away. If coming by bus, it is the fast-track bus route A between Dartford centre (and station) to Greenhithe and Bluewater.

www.thebridgedartford. co.uk

133 Shorne Marshes

▶ HOW TO GET THERE

Shorne Marshes [TQ693745]

This reserve is reached by walking along the Saxon Shore Way from Gravesend (distance from Gravesend Station is 3 miles). Gravesend has the nearest car parks, road access and public transport. Cyclists can use the Sustrans cycle track which runs alongside the Thames and Medway Canal to the south of the reserve. Open at all times.

www.rspb.org.uk/reserves/
guide/s/shornemarshes

*The lonely landscape
at Shorne Marshes*

Shorne Marshes are one of several areas along the Thames where the space and isolation was used for military purposes – a firing range here, explosive factory at Wat Tyler (south Essex) and artillery at Shoeburyness. Shorne Marshes are now a RSPB reserve, having been sold by the Ministry of Defence in 2000. There are 385 acres of pastures and saltmarsh. Controlling the flow of water in the ditches, cutting back hawthorn bushes, and fencing the grazing areas have improved the habitat for birdlife. The numbers of breeding redshanks and over-wintering ducks have increased since 2000. There are bearded tits and Ceti's warblers in the reeds, and water voles and great crested newts in the ditches.

It is rather a lonely place because the only way to reach it is by walking from Gravesend, Cliffe Pools or Higham. The Saxon Shore Way along the top of the seawall allows you to watch the river and mudflats as well as the fields. The path bends around saltmarshes and creeks, which are feeding grounds for birds when the tide is out. One of the large bends is around Higham Bight, where you may see teal feeding on the mud in winter.

At Gravesend, the Saxon Shore Way goes past the dock that was the entrance to the Medway Canal, and next to the boatyards of the Port of London Authority. But when these are behind you there are no pubs or other facilities until you reach Cliffe, or leave the seawall to walk into Higham.

134 Cliffe Pools Nature Reserve

Cliffe Pools Nature Reserve offers a landscape of small lakes and big skies. There are nature trails that cross the reserve, offering great views of the pools, wildlife and the River Thames which runs alongside. During the spring and autumn migration periods there is an excellent chance to see some rare birds. Big flocks of ducks and grebes also gather at this time. Hen harriers and other birds of prey are regular visitors. In summer, breeding redshanks, avocets and common terns may be seen, with nightingales and turtle doves singing from the bushes.

There are six viewing points at fresh pools and saline lagoons. The Pinnacle Viewpoint gives excellent views over the reserve and the Thames Estuary, and trails from the reserve lead to the banks of the Thames. Recently, silt from Tilbury Docks has been added to the lagoons to make shallows for waders to feed. More will be added to make nesting islands.

 HOW TO GET THERE

Cliffe Pools Nature Reserve [TQ723770]

From the A289 follow the signs for Wainscott and Cliffe onto the B2000. Take the Lower Rochester Road (B2000) signposted Cliffe and Cooling. At the crossroads, turn left (signposted Higham). Before you enter Cliffe village, take the second left after the Cliffe village sign (into Rectory Road). Turn right at the next T-junction and, after $1/3$ mile, turn left into Salt Lane. Continue along Salt Lane to the car park on the left-hand side after a sharp right bend. National Cycle Network Route 179 and the Saxon Shore Way pass through Cliffe. If travelling by bus, the 133 bus from Rochester stops at Cliffe. The reserve is open at all times, but the car park is open only from 8.30am to 5pm.

www.rspb.org.uk/reserves/ guide/c/cliffepools/about. aspx

Cliffe Pools Nature Reserve

135 Northward Hill

HOW TO GET THERE

Northward Hill [TQ768765]

RSPB Northward Hill, Bromhey Farm, Cooling, Rochester, Kent ME3 8DS. There is a car park by the Visitor Centre. The Saxon Shore Way passes through the reserve, and National Cycle Network Route 179 passes through High Halstow. The nearest station is Strood Railway Station; there are trains approximately every hour from London. The nearest bus stop is in High Halstow, and there are hourly buses from Strood to High Halstow village. Walk west along the Cooling Road for approximately one mile.

www.rspb.org.uk/reserves/guide/n/northwardhill

Overlooking the north Kent Marshes, Northward Hill combines woodland and marshes. It is well established, having been owned and expanded by the RSPB since 1956. The mixture of grassland, grazing marsh and bramble scrub set among cherry and pear orchards make it one of Europe's top places for birds. The woodland is famous for being the UK's largest heronry, with more than 150 pairs.

In spring, turtle doves, nightingales and warblers join breeding woodpeckers and tits, and the grasslands come alive with grasshoppers, crickets and spiders. The marshes and rough pastures are breeding grounds for avocets, lapwings and redshank – which of course attract marsh harriers that hunt along the north Kent coast.

There are four walking trails, varying in length from half a mile to 4 miles.

There is a visitor centre with a full programme of teaching and organised tours. Cliffe Pools are close if you want to visit two places in one day.

Northward Hill

136

Motney Hill and Nor Marsh

Motney Hill is a narrow peninsula, with 62 acres of saltmarsh surrounded by mudflats, that juts into the Medway Estuary towards Nor Marsh. Nor Marsh is an island made up of saltmarsh (190 acres) that can be viewed from Motney and the Riverside Country Park, but has no public access. These isolated places provide safe areas for birds to feed and breed in an increasingly developed estuary.

The saltmarsh and mudflats here are important for migrating and wintering birds. Both sites have black-tailed godwits on migration. Shelducks, pintail ducks, grey plovers and turnstones over-winter on Nor Marsh, and great crested grebes and knots at Motney. Less common ducks including goldeneyes and red-breasted mergansers are seen regularly. Rarities include black-necked and Slavonian grebes. In spring and summer, birds nesting on the saltmarsh islands include avocets, redshanks and ringed plovers, with increasing numbers of black-headed gulls.

You cannot actually go onto the reserves themselves, but you can get good views from the Saxon Shore Way footpath. There are no facilities at the reserves, but there is a full range in the Riverside Country Park run by Medway Borough Council.

HOW TO GET THERE

Motney Hill and Nor Marsh [TQ825681]

Motney Hill and Nor Marsh are near Gillingham, Kent. From the A2 in Gillingham, take the A289, signposted to Riverside Country Park. From National Cycle Network Route 1, take West Motney Way. The park is in Lower Rainham Road and there is a car park after 200 yards. Nor Marsh can be viewed from the car park. To get to Motney Hill, walk along the Saxon Shore Way eastwards for 2½ miles. The nearest railway station is Rainham (Kent). There are buses from Gillingham to the Riverside Country Park.

www.rspb.org.uk/reserves/guide/n/normarsh/index.aspx

Motney Hill

137 Elmley Marshes

HOW TO GET THERE

Elmley Marshes [TQ938680]

Near Queensborough, Isle of Sheppey, Kent ME12 3RW. From the M2, Junction 5, take the A249 towards Sheerness. When on the Isle of Sheppey follow the signs for RSPB Elmley Marshes at the first roundabout. There is a 2 mile track from the entrance to the car park through the western side of the marshes, and a further mile to walk to the closest bird hide – wide open spaces! The Saxon Shore Way comes closest at Kingsferry Bridge. National Cycle Network Route 1 passes the track to the reserve. The nearest train stations are at Swale and Queensborough (7 miles). If you are coming by boat, there are visitor moorings available at Queensborough.

www.rspb.org.uk/reserves/guide/e/elmleymarshes
email: northkentmarshes@rspb.org.uk

Elmley Marshes, managed by the RSPB, is a wide expanse of grassland and pools with the highest density of breeding waders in southern England. It is well known for winter sightings of wildfowl from Siberia, eastern Europe and Scandinavia; more than 20,000 wigeons, 5,000 teals, and pintail in their hundreds, plus Bewick's swans, white-fronted geese, red-breasted mergansers and various species of grebe. There can be several hundred grey plovers and black-tailed godwits and several thousand dunlins among the waders roosting here. Peregrines, hen harriers and short-eared owls hunt over the marshes. In summer, the avocets defend their young from harriers by flying around the predators, calling loudly. The elegance of the avocets is transformed into parental fury.

There are two nature trails. One is a 6 mile round trip to the furthest hide; the other is a 2 mile walk, visiting two bird hides.

Elmley Marshes

Did you know...
Dolphins and porpoises use the Thames Estuary and can be seen in the summer and autumn months.

138

Swale National Nature Reserve

On the Isle of Sheppey, the Swale is a National Nature Reserve on a coastal strip of 540 acres between Harty Ferry and Shell Ness. The Swale reserve is valued for its plants (eel grass, Ray's knotgrass, white seakale and samphire) which support uncommon butterflies and moths. For visitors in spring and early summer, there are breeding birds, particularly waders. In winter, look for ducks, geese and waders on the shore and in the sea.

If you park at Shell Ness, you will enjoy the 2 mile walk along the seawall. This allows you to look at the reedbeds and dykes on one side and the saltmarsh on the other. In 2012, the bird hide by the seawall was closed for repairs, but hopefully it will be available again in 2013.

On the way to the Swale National Nature Reserve, on the B2231 road between Eastchurch and Leysdown, you will see a road to Harty Ferry with a brown tourism sign to Raptors View Point at Capel Fleet [TR022681]. This View Point is a raised mound with information boards and a car park where you get a chance to see harriers gliding over the marshes.

There is an 8 mile circular walk along the seawall from Leysdown Country Park to the Swale National Nature Reserve that returns by Sayes Court to get onto the cycle track that is part of the Isle of Harty Trail. This trail passes within half a mile of Raptors View Point.

 HOW TO GET THERE

Swale National Nature Reserve [TR051682]

The Swale National Nature Reserve is at the eastern end of the Isle of Sheppey, in a part that used to be called the Isle of Harty. On crossing to Sheppey by the A249, take the B2231 at the first roundabout, signposted to Leysdown-on-Sea. Go through Leysdown-on-Sea, following signs to the beach and Leysdown Coastal Park. The road becomes a track, and there are several parking places on the way to Shell Ness, where there is a small car park close to the reserve. A footpath goes from Harty Ferry to Shell Ness via Sayes Court Farm. There is a bus service to Leysdown from Minster, but no other public transport. If coming by boat, there is a good anchorage at Harty Ferry, and a landing place by the Ferry Inn.

www.naturalengland.org.uk/ourwork/conservation/designations/nnr/1006143.aspx

Do not confuse nature reserves with naturist beaches: both are present at Shell Ness!

► HOW TO GET THERE

Oare Marshes [TR013647]

Church Road, Oare, Faversham ME13 0QA. From the A2 road, take the B2045 to Oare. Turn left, cross the river, and turn right to go past Oare Church. Continue north until you reach a car park at the end of the road by the seawall. There is a car park reserved for the disabled less than ¼ mile from a bird hide overlooking the East Flood. The Saxon Shore Way runs around the reserve beside the Swale and Faversham Creek. If coming by bus, the 333 service runs from Faversham and Sittingbourne to Oare village, which is about 1½ miles from the reserve. If coming by boat, there is open anchorage at Harty Ferry.

www.kentwildlifetrust.org.uk/reserves/oare-marshes

139 Oare Marshes

Oare Marshes is a birdwatchers' paradise, especially for those who cannot walk long distances. Compared with the expanse of the other reserves along the Swale, Oare is a compact place to visit. The total size is 200 acres, but the part that most visitors see, the East Flood, is only a fraction of the reserve. If you walk up onto the seawall near the car park, you get a good view of the East Flood, the hides, the paths and the concentrations of birds. The reserve has fields, freshwater dykes, open water scrapes, a seawall and a saltmarsh. The habitat is kept suitable as wetland by adjusting water levels and by livestock grazing. Like the other reserves beside the Thames Estuary, it is of international importance for migratory, over-wintering and breeding wetland birds.

The breeding birds include avocet, redshank, snipe, lapwing, water rail, common tern and garganey. Black-tailed godwit, ruff, little stint, curlew, sandpiper and whimbrel come on their migrations. In winter, Brent geese, dunlins, curlews, wigeons, merlins, hen harriers, short-eared owls, and the occasional bittern, can be seen. In spring, you may hear odd croaking sounds from the ditches, where large marsh frogs lurk. Marsh frogs are the largest native frogs in Britain, about 4 inches long – making a large meal for a heron or grass snake.

*Birdwatchers at
Oare Marshes*

140

South Swale Nature Reserve

South Swale Nature Reserve is large reserve (1,000 acres), visited by thousands of wildfowl and waders in winter. In summer, the sound of beetles, grasshoppers, skylark, reed warbler and redshank will be entrancing. You may hear the 'ching' of a bearded reedling (bearded tit) in the reeds or see a marsh harrier wheeling around the sky. Throughout the year, you are likely to hear larks and to see waders along the shore.

The reserve is explored by walking along the seawall. Whether you walk on top of the wall on the foreshore, or on the inland side, there is plenty to see. Yellow horned-poppy adorn the beach. The saltmarsh plants, golden samphire, sea purslane and sea lavender, grow on the marshy area that bulges out into the Swale. On the landward side, look for the wild carrot and the short spiny rest harrow. While you may visit this reserve by walking the Saxon Shore Way, many visitors and their dogs are happy with the walk along the Swale shore and back again.

There is a pub at the corner in Seasalter Road, where you can park. Or you may like to go into Faversham before visiting Oare Marshes on the other (west) side of Faversham Creek.

HOW TO GET THERE

South Swale Nature Reserve [TR060643]

Graveney, near Faversham CT5 4BP. The reserve lies to the north of Graveney Marshes and alongside Faversham Creek. If coming by car, from Brenley Corner roundabout (the junction of the M2, A2 and A299) take the minor road to Graveney, then continue past Graveney for another 2 miles along Seasalter Road to a bend by the Sportsman Inn and beach huts on the seawall. Cars can be parked on the road verge near the Inn and seawall, but not in the Inn's car park unless you are a patron. Enter the reserve by the Saxon Shore Way on the seawall going westward to Faversham. If coming on foot, join the Saxon Shore Way in Faversham (the nearest train station) and walk for 5 miles beside Faversham Creek to reach the reserve. The walk through the reserve is another 3 miles. You will by now be ready for refreshment in the Sportsman Inn and a bus ride back to Faversham. The bus service from Canterbury to Whitstable goes via Faversham and Seasalter.

www.kentwildlifetrust.org.uk/reserves/south-swale

Foreshore at South Swale Nature Reserve

Oare ···· Teynham ···· Conyer ···· Oare Marshes Reserve ···· East Fleet ···· Oare

10 MILES A circular walk that explores the Oare Marshes and shows Kent as the Garden of England is made by combining the Saxon Shore Way and the Swale Heritage Trail. When plans for a reserve at the old brickworks at Conyer bear fruit, it will meet our aspiration of linking two or more reserves. It offers interest, wildlife and solitude, and is loveliest in spring when the blossom is out in the orchards. For those who travel here by public transport, we suggest the bridge at Oare Creek as the starting point, since it is within walking distance, or a bus ride from the centre of Faversham. Another starting point is the car park at Oare Marshes, which is where you might land if you had come by boat and anchored at Harty Ferry.

As you will be using well-marked footpaths, it should be easy to follow in either direction – your choice may depend on the direction of the wind and the weather forecast (the top of the seawall is exposed). Going clockwise, and starting at Oare Creek Bridge, walk up the street past the Three Mariners pub through Oare (northwest) to the road junction of Uplees Road and Colegates Road. About 100 yards along Uplees Road, take the footpath through a kissing gate on the left side to cross a field. The path goes through several fields, a farm, and one more field to a lane, where you turn right. After half a mile, the lane turns left around a house (a former pub) called 'The Mounted Rifleman'. Shortly after this corner, take the footpath on the right through a field and past an orchard. At a tarmac track (a private road), continue straight across to the footpath by a conifer hedge. After more orchards, you come to a lane, Deerton Street. The new orchards look very smart and efficient, but the old neglected ones are havens for wildlife, with knurled trunks, nettles and freedom from pesticides. At Deerton Street, turn right and follow the lane which will lead you to Conyer. You will pass a natural burial ground, which is a peaceful place for a short meditative break in the walk. Where the lane bends right, look for a footpath going straight ahead; this cuts across a loop in the lane, which is named Teynham Street. Teynham Church is a pretty sight on a small hill and can be visited via a footpath through an orchard. Continue along the lane, into Conyer, a small village that was once a busy port with brickworks.

In Conyer, the main street goes down a small hill to a meeting of several paths. Turn right in the street called 'The Quay'. This is

Teynham Levels

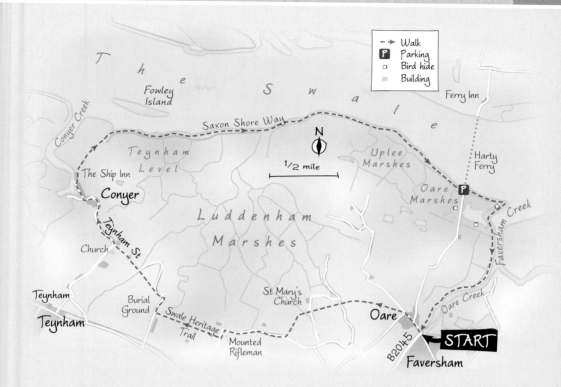

	Walk
P	Parking
□	Bird hide
▪	Building

clearly signposted as the Saxon Shore Way. As you are at the halfway point of your walk, you may be ready for lunch at the Ship Inn, along this street. The Saxon Shore Way goes past a new residential block called the North Quay, and beside the site of the former brickworks. This site is now overgrown with scrub and marsh plants, and it is intended that it should become a nature reserve. Once you reach the seawall, the route is obvious – turn right to walk eastwards along the seawall until you get to Oare Marshes Reserve and the slipway of Harty Ferry. Fowley Island, used by black-headed gulls as a breeding site, is the low marsh in the middle of the Swale. You are likely to see avocets, curlews, redshanks and shelducks as you walk, but you will rarely see other people.

On reaching the Oare Marshes Reserve, the simplest route is to stay on the seawall to the point at the entrance of Faversham Creek where a bird hide offers a resting place out of the wind. Alternatively, you can go along the lane on the west side of East Fleet and the path on the south side to get a closer look at the birds on this expanse of shallow water. Either way, the walk finishes by walking beside Oare Creek to get back to the starting point.

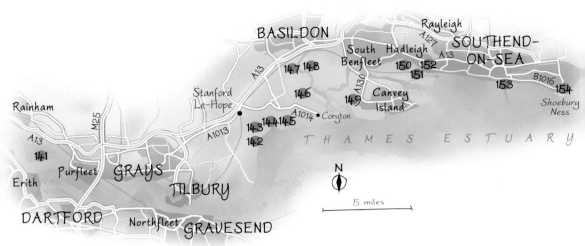

11. South Essex

The tidal mudflats and saltmarshes in South Essex are major wildlife habitats, attracting large numbers of ducks, geese and waders in winter. There is much more to see though than simply the birdlife. Wildflowers are good at colonising the impoverished soils of old industrial sites, and these attract insects and reptiles. Going from small to large, you may see seals basking on the sandbanks off Southend and you may see dolphins or porpoises. Although there are major riverside industries, most especially on Canvey Island, there are wide open spaces all around. The Thames Estuary Coastal Path is planned to extend the well-established path beside the shore at Southend along the Essex shore to London and link with the Thames Path and the Saxon Shore Way.

The tidal estuary is a marine fish nursery for the North Sea stocks of dover sole, sea bass, oyster, cockle fisheries, prawns, perch, thick-lipped mullet and the five-bearded rockling. Fish numbers for dace and bream have increased in recent years, as have shad and smelt, which are particularly sensitive to pollution. Small numbers of salmon and sea trout annually migrate to and from the Thames.

Southend Pier

141

Rainham Marshes Nature Reserve

 HOW TO GET THERE

Rainham Marshes Nature Reserve [TQ534802]

New Tank Hill Road, Purfleet, Essex RM19 1SZ. If coming by road, turn off the A13 at the Aveley, Wennington and Purfleet junction onto the A1306 between Rainham and Lakeside, head for Purfleet, and take the A1090, New Tank Hill Road. Look for the brown signs. Rainham Marshes is on National Cycle Network Route 13 and the Thames Estuary Coastal Path. The nearest train station is Purfleet. If coming by bus, it is Ensign bus route 44 between Lakeside and Orsett Hospital, Grays.

www.rspb.org.uk/rainham

Rainham Marshes Nature Reserve is a wetland and grassland habitat with small woodlands next to the River Thames. It was acquired in 2000 by the RSPB, having been a military range closed to the public for over 100 years. The impressive visitor centre has a teaching facility, café, shop and toilets. Access around the reserve is good, with ramps and boardwalks covering a 2 mile circular route. For those who want a longer walk, the seawall is part of the London Loop. There is a children's adventure playground, a separate toddler play area, and plenty of picnic places.

The architectural bird hides have amazing views of wetland habitat and species – come here to see lots of lapwings and the marsh harriers and little egrets. It is a sanctuary for water voles, and there are interesting spiders along the seawall. Rainham has a busy calendar of activities, and there are plenty of opportunities for volunteering with the Essex Wildlife Trust and the RSPB.

Rainham Marshes and bird hide

Visitor centre at Thurrock Thameside Nature Park

142 Thurrock Thameside Nature Park

This large new nature park has been created on the banks of the Thames near Stanford-Le-Hope in Thurrock, with coastal mudflats and saltmarshes. The habitats include Thames Terrace grasslands, old and new woodlands, hedgerows, ponds and reedbeds. The park opened in 2012, and has a large circular visitor centre that offers spectacular views of the Thames. Educational and volunteer activities take place in this 'low-carbon' cedar wood building. There are numerous footpaths, bird hides, and a bridleway within the present 120 acre site – the site will extend to 654 acres by 2016. The visitor centre and some of the bird hides are accessible for wheelchairs and pushchairs. There are already 50 species of waders in the reserve, together with lizards, great crested newts and slow worms.

The Thurrock Thameside Nature Park has transformed the former landfill site in Mucking. With the adjacent Stanford Warren, it forms a 1,500 acre diverse wildlife habitat, adding to a chain of reserves from Shoeburyness to the outskirts of London.

When complete, this nature park will provide a continuous green space that links communities via footpaths, bridleways and cycle paths. In the future it will be linked by the Thames Estuary Coastal Path to Tilbury to the west and Wat Tyler Country Park to the east.

 HOW TO GET THERE

Thurrock Thameside Nature Park [TR696806]

Mucking, Stanford-Le-Hope, Thurrock, Essex SS17 0RN. From the A13 take the A31013 at Orsett Cock Roundabout, signed to Stanford-Le-Hope. Turn left into Buckingham Hill Road and right into Mucking Wharf Road. Go past the welcome signs along a single-track road until you reach the reserve entrance and car park. The Thames Estuary Coastal Path is being extended to this new park. From the train station at Stanford-le-Hope, walk through Stanford Warren reserve to Mucking Wharf (about a mile).

www.essexwt.org.uk/visitor_
centres__nature_reserves/
thurrock_thameside_nature_
park

143 Stanford Warren

▶ HOW TO GET THERE

Stanford Warren [TQ687812], Mucking Mudflats and Earls Hope Salt Marsh

Mucking Wharf Road, Stanford-le-Hope. From the A1013, turn left at the first traffic lights, and then right, south, down Butts Lane. Look for a turning on the left into Mucking Wharf Road. There is roadside parking by the former church from where a footpath enters Stanford Warren. If coming by train, turn right outside Stanford Station and right down Wharf Road. After the bridge under the railway is a footpath into Stanford Warren. Buses run from Basildon to Stanford Station.

www.essexwt.org.uk/visitor_centres__nature_reserves/stanford_warren_nature_reserve/
www.thurrock.gov.uk/planning/environment/content.php?page=stanford_marshes

Once an area of gravel pits, Stanford Warren has become one of the larger reedbeds in Essex. With the adjacent Mucking Mudflats and Earls Hope Salt Marsh, there is a large expanse of varied habitats. In spring and summer the reedbeds are full of reed buntings, reed warblers and sedge warblers, which breed here. Cuckoos take advantage and lay their eggs in warblers' nests. Shy water rail also lurk among the reeds. In winter there are bearded tits, grey wagtail and snipe along the Hassenbrooke, a small river that runs through the Warren. Some tracks are suitable for horse riding and there are also some angling lakes. The reserve is open at all times and is a good place for seeing water voles.

Reedbeds at Stanford Warren

144 Mucking Mudflats

When you have finished admiring the reedbeds at Stanford
Warren and trying to identify warblers by their song, you can
walk down to the seawall to watch waders and ducks feeding
on the Mucking Mudflats. The mudflats get their name from
the nearby village of Mucking, and not from the nature of the
mud, which is no more messy than any other Essex mud. The
village name may be derived from 'Mucca', the name of a Saxon
chieftain. Whatever the derivation of the name, there is a large
bay with a seawall on three sides, where you can get good views
of birds when the tide is out.

145

Earls Hope Salt Marsh

Earls Hope is reached via Stanford Warren (page 208). If you walk along the seawall from Sandford Warren, past Mucking Mudflats and towards the oil refineries on Canvey Island, you will come to a place where the path veers towards dry land. In front of you is the Earls Hope Salt Marsh, where sea lavender, sea purslane and sea asters grow. This is a true saltmarsh that is covered by the sea at high tide, and summer is a good time to visit when the sea lavender makes a purple haze. There is no easy route through or round the saltmarsh, so when you have finished exploring, return the way you came to get back to Stanford.

HOW TO GET THERE

Fobbing Marsh [TQ716845]

Fobbing Marsh is on the west side of Holehaven Creek and south of Basildon. To get to Fobbing Marsh, park on the road in Fobbing and find Marsh Lane. Walk down the lane to a junction of footpaths. The path straight ahead, through a gate and across a field, will bring you to Fobbing Marsh, designated with a sign board on a metal gate. There is a footpath, marked with white posts, that goes to Vange Marsh. There is a bus service from Basildon to Stanford-Le-Hope that stops in Fobbing.

www.essexwt.org.uk/visitor_centres__nature_reserves/fobbing_marsh

Did you know...
There are at least
60 active shipping
terminals on the
tidal Thames.

146

Fobbing Marsh

Fobbing Marsh is remote, requiring a long walk down tracks and across fields. From the entrance, marked by a board on a field gate, there is a path under the pylons to a seawall by Vange Creek. The wildlife is similar to Vange Marsh (see page 212) and the two reserves make a large and valuable green space. If you visit, you are likely to be on your own. The marshes are always open.

Fobbing Marsh

Ponies help to control the reeds and other plants at Vange Marsh

HOW TO GET THERE

Vange Marsh Nature Reserve [TQ731873]

The easiest way to get to Vange Marsh is to start at Wat Tyler Country Park (see page 213). Leave your car in the car park and walk back along Pitsea Hall Lane to the railway crossing. After crossing the railway, look for a gravel track between a house and a yard entrance on the left side, opposite the station car park. There was no footpath sign when visited, but this track is a public footpath. Go down the track until you are under the flyover of the A13 road, and you will find a footpath crossing the railway line – take care on crossing. Across the railway, turn right and you will come to an entrance into Vange Marsh. There is a footpath marked with white posts through the fields to Fobbing Marsh. Pitsea train station and buses to Pitsea are both convenient for Vange.

www.rspb.org.uk/reserves/ guide/v/vangemarsh/

147 Vange Marsh

Vange Marsh is a mosaic of wetland habitats, maintained by controlling water levels and by grazing. The part near Pitsea is accessible, and the more distant part to the south is reached by following a footpath around fields. Freshwater and saltwater lagoons attract breeding avocets, common terns, little ringed plovers, lapwings and reed buntings. In winter, wigeons, teals and shovelers visit the site, and bearded tits thrive in the reedbeds. Ponies are used to graze the grass and control the reeds. Scarce emerald damselflies buzz around the reserve in summer. The site has a population of adders, and barn owls can be spotted hunting over the marshes.

The managers of Vange (RSPB) and Fobbing (Essex Wildlife Trust) are grateful for help from volunteers.

148
Wat Tyler Country Park

The Wat Tyler Country Park is set in the South Essex Marshes on the site of a former explosives factory. The South Essex Marshes are managed by the RSPB and they have a visitor centre in the country park.

The park is very good for birdwatching all year round, and the RSPB give a free guided walk each Thursday (see the website in the box on the right for details, the seasonal highlights and most recent sightings).

There are two large bird hides in the country park, with keys that can be bought at the Wat Tyler Centre or borrowed from the RSPB visitor centre. Three screen hides give good views of the tidal creek.

This country park has much to entertain visitors: a museum and information boards about the explosives factory, a playground, a miniature railway, a village scene, and nearly 2 miles of trails accessible for wheelchairs and pushchairs.

Volunteer activities are arranged by the RSPB.

 HOW TO GET THERE

Wat Tyler Country Park [TQ737863]

Pitsea Hall Lane, Pitsea, Basildon, Essex SS16 4UH. Pitsea Hall Lane is a turning off the Pitsea roundabout beneath a flyover on the A13. There is free entry and parking at Wat Tyler Country Park. It closes at 5pm. It is close to the Thames Estuary Coastal Path and National Cycle Network Route 16. For trains and buses, you arrive at Pitsea, a mile away. If you are coming by boat, mooring is possible for small craft at the marina on Holehaven Creek at the end of the Wat Tyler Park.

www.rspb.org.uk/reserves/ guide/s/southessexmarshes/ index.aspx

The village at the Wat Tyler Centre

149 West Canvey Marsh

 HOW TO GET THERE

West Canvey Marsh
[TQ776842]

From the A13, take the A130 to a roundabout junction of Canvey Road and Roscommon Way. It is open at all times, but the free car park closes from 5pm to 9am. It is near the Thames Estuary Coastal Path and National Cycle Network Route 16. The nearest train station is Benfleet, 4 miles away.

http://www.rspb.org. uk/reserves/guide/w/ westcanveymarsh/index. aspx

West Canvey Marsh is the largest single area of green space on Canvey Island, and is part of the South Essex Marshes. This wetland includes nearly 2 miles of nature trails, three viewing points, and a picnic and adventure area for children. The viewing points are open-backed bird hides, which offer some shelter from the rain and wind. A Radar key is needed for wheelchairs at a kissing gate. Most of the paths have firm surfaces. Dogs are restricted to one circular path, and must be kept on a lead. The longest path in the reserve leads to the seawall, overlooking East Haven Creek. From here, a footpath runs round the western edge of Canvey Island. Despite the oil refinery on the southern skyline, there is a sense of open space and countryside.

Adventure area at West Canvey Marsh

150

Hadleigh Castle Country Park

The idea of a country park at Hadleigh was conceived in the 1930s, but it was not enacted until the 1970s, as an alternative to golf courses and housing estates. Even in the 1990s, active conservation was needed to stop a main road being built across the park. All this is reminiscent of Hadleigh Castle, built in 1230–2 by Henry III as a defence against a French invasion. Hadleigh Castle and the surrounding farmlands were bought by the Salvation Army in 1891, to make a colony for poor people from London. The colony thrived on brickworks and market gardening until 1914, but thereafter declined, and the ruins were added to the country park in 1971.

The park is one of the largest in Essex, 450 acres in area. The higher part lies along an escarpment of London Clay and is now mostly wooded, with small meadows and ponds. The castle was built on the edge of the escarpment – rather too close to the edge in fact, because the walls began to slide down the slope within a few years. There is an area of sandy soil near the former brickworks, and large expanses of pasture and marshland on the lower side of the park, near Benfleet Creek. Therefore the park has a variety of habitats, which is reflected in the wildlife found within it. The species of wildlife are listed on the park's website, and are broadly representative of South Essex countryside.

There are footpaths and bridleways around the park, with a selection of marked trails. The longer trails (60 and 90 minutes long) go down the slope from the main car park and are rough and muddy in places. Extending the walk you can explore the ruins of the castle, or reach Leigh-on-Sea – well worth a visit for a fish meal.

Close to the car park is a teaching centre and a Saxon-style roundhouse built from wood, reed and clay.

⊙ HOW TO GET THERE

Hadleigh Castle Country Park [TQ800872]

By road, the main entrance and car park is in Chapel Lane, Hadleigh SS7 2PP. Chapel Lane is a turning off the London Road (A13), marked with brown signs to the Country Park. Or you can walk or cycle along the seawall on the southern part of the park, which is reached by going along Ferry Road and past the moored boats. The seawall route goes all the way to Leigh-on-Sea and Two Tree Island. If coming by train, Benfleet Station is close to the western end of the park. From the station, you can enter the main park by a bridleway from St Mary's Road. For buses, the nearest stop is on the corner of Chapel Lane and London Road.

www.hadleighcountrypark. co.uk

Hadleigh Castle

Two Tree Island

HOW TO GET THERE

Two Tree Island, Leigh
[TQ825853]

Leigh on Sea, Essex. From
the A13, take a turning to
Leigh Station; and from Leigh
Station, take the lane over
the railway bridge for about
a mile over Leigh Creek onto
Two Tree Island. There is a
car park on the left (east)
side soon after the bridge.
Another is at the end of the
lane on the south shore.
Two Tree Island is open at all
times. From National Cycle
Network Route 16 and the
Thames Estuary Coastal Path,
take the lane at Leigh Station
as described above. For
trains, the C2C service from
Fenchurch Station in London
to Southend stops at Leigh.
Buses go from Southend to
Old Leigh. If you are coming
by boat you can moor at
Leigh, and dinghies can land
at the slipway on the south
shore (by the car park).

www.essexwt.org.uk/visitor_
centres__nature_reserves/
two_tree_island

151 Two Tree Island, Leigh

The island, named after two elm trees that blew down in the
1960s, is a mixture of grassland, scrub, reedbed, lagoons and
saltmarsh.

Saltmarsh plants include sea purslane, common sea lavender,
sea arrow grass, common saltmarsh grass and sea aster. The
mudflats have beds of eel grass which feed thousands of Brent
geese in winter. Curlew, dunlin, redshank and grey plover, short-
eared owl, skylark and meadow pipit are present all year.

Other creatures on the island include carder bees, butterflies
(marbled white, small skipper and Essex skipper), slow worms,
adders and common lizards.

Please keep to the footpaths, which give good walks around
the island.

Volunteers meet monthly, arranged by the Essex Wildlife
Trust.

Other reserves nearby are Southend foreshore, Belton Hills
and West Canvey Marsh.

152 Belton Hills

A vital haven for wildflowers and invertebrates, Belton Hills has a number of rare species, including the Deptford Pink. Despite its proximity to the railway line and the suburbs of Leigh and Southend, it is a hillside crawling with wildlife. This reserve, which commands stunning views out across the adjacent Two Tree Island, is considered of 'national significance', with more than 667 invertebrate species recorded, including the rare shrill carder bee, found in just seven other areas of the UK. It is worth climbing up the steps from the station to enjoy the views across the estuary.

There are paths running across the hillside, inviting you to explore the 63 acres of the reserve.

Below Belton Hills, on the coastal side of the railway, is the fishing port of Old Leigh-on-Sea. This is the place to buy fish or eat in one of the pubs and cafés.

 HOW TO GET THERE

Belton Hills [TQ832858]

Marine Parade, Leigh-on-Sea. The Thames Estuary Coastal Path and National Cycle Network Route 16 run along the seafront. For trains, it is the C2C service to Leigh Station – Belton Hills is the green space on the hillside above the station. Car parking is allowed along the roadside near the station. If coming by boat, moor at Leigh-on-Sea.

www.wildessex.net/sites/ Belton Hills.htm

The Thames Estuary from Belton Hills

153 Southend Foreshore

It may come as a surprise to some to think of Southend as a wildlife haven, but it is a great place to see migrating birds, especially at Southend pier. The foreshore and mudflats are the winter home for Brent geese, dunlin, teal, mallard, widgeon, ringer plover, turnstone and godwits, and a good time to watch birds is when the tide comes in. The birds retreat along the waterline in great numbers, moving towards Two Tree Island at Leigh, which is the last part of the foreshore to be covered by the rising tide.

The concrete seawall has some of the saltmarsh plants, like sea thrift, sea beet and sea purslane, and look for the golden samphire that flowers from July to September. The beach at Southend is one of the best places in the Thames Estuary to explore rock pools – searching for sea anemones, sea squirts, sponges, sea gooseberries, seaweeds and small fish. When the tide is out, seals bask on the sandbanks.

Behind the promenade there are several areas of rough grass and bushes: Belton Hills Local Nature Reserve at Leigh, Cliff Gardens at Westcliffe, Gunners Park at Shoeburyness. At Chalkwell, Crow Stone marks the traditional limit of the river.

Southend foreshore at low tide

154

Gunners Park, Shoeburyness

Shoeburyness is the point at which the north side of the Thames Estuary turns to become the shore of the North Sea. It was a place of military importance from Roman times until the middle of the 20th century. While it was used for weapons testing, wildlife had the benefit of space with restricted human access. When the Ministry of Defence sold the land in 2000, a condition was made that a large open space would be retained with public access. The result is a large (84 acres) semi-wild park by the sea, with a small lake, grassland, and a reserve that has been fenced off while it is being restored. There are stark concrete reminders of the past, but the natural grassland and scrub provide habitats for a variety of wildlife. The soil is sandy and poor in nutrients, which suits clovers and saxifrages. The foreshore has pebbles near the seawall, but stretches out as a large expanse of sand at low tide – providing more feeding grounds for birds. There are car parks and places for children to play, and National Cycle Network Route 16 passes through the park.

HOW TO GET THERE

Gunners Park, Shoeburyness [TR030905]

Campfield Road/Ness Road, Shoeburyness. The Thames Estuary Coastal Path and National Cycle Network Route 16 run along the seafront. If coming by train, the C2C service has stations at Leigh, Southend and Shoeburyness. The train allows you to return to where you started walking or cycling.

www.southend.gov.
uk/info/200073/parks_
and_open_spaces/44/
parks_gardens_and_nature_
reserves/10
Southend-on-Sea

Old fortifications and a new cycle path at Shoeburyness

Crow Stone

linear walk

Shoeburyness ···· Gunners Park ····
Southend ···· Westcliffe ···· Leigh-on-Sea

7½ MILES We have not found a circular walk that links several reserves in Essex, but there is a good linear walk that satisfies the theme that the Thames is a chain of wildlife habitats. This walk can be done in either direction, and the length can be adjusted by selecting different stations. Starting at Shoeburyness and finishing at Leigh-on-Sea is the easiest way.

Shoeburyness is the end of the railway line from Fenchurch Street Station in London, but all the stations in Essex have car parks if you decide to catch a train elsewhere.

From Shoeburyness Station, go out of the forecourt to the road. Across the road is a footpath to the seafront with a play area for children, a car park and the first of many notice boards about the natural history of the seashore. On the seafront, turn right along Rampart Terrace to a path on the seaward side of a row of modern houses. This emerges into a square, with a park on the far side; this is the start of Gunners Park. Along the small road in front of the restored houses, you come to an open space with several paths to take you westwards. From this point on, the route for walkers is beside the seawall until you get to Leigh-on-Sea.

Depending on the state of the tide, the weather and your interests, you may prefer to get onto the beach and walk over the sand and shingle – but there are some parts of the seafront around the pier where human activity dominates. Soon after passing the pier, look at the gardens at Westcliffe, because there is a fenced area that has been allowed to grow

Crunching along the pebbles on the foreshore

Hadleigh
London Road
SOUTHEND-ON-SEA
Hadleigh Castle
Belton Hills
Leigh-on-Sea
Chalkwell
Westcliff
Southend Central
Southend Victoria
Southend East
Thorpe Bay
START
Two Tree Island
Crow Stone
Thorpe Esplanade
Shoeburyness
Southend Pier

N

- → Walk
- P Parking
- ■ Building

1 mile

T H A M E S   E S T U A R Y

wild. Further west, the seashore is spacious at low tide. After the Crow Stone, the seafront promenade becomes a narrow path between the railway and several sailing clubs until you get to the old fishing port of Leigh. Pubs, fish restaurants and art galleries may delay you, but walking on beside the railway will bring you to the station. It is worth summoning up the energy to climb the steps of Belton Hills above the station to get a great view across the estuary. If you have time, walk back to the station and along the lane to Two Tree Island – a place where you might have parked your car. For those who want to walk further, another 3 miles through Hadleigh Castle Country Park will bring you to Benfleet Station (10½ miles from Shoeburyness). Cyclists will find that the route starts along the shared paths, and continues along the road before having to walk from the Crow Stone to Leigh.

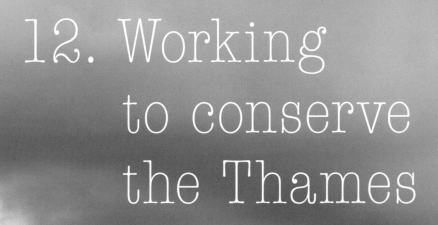

12. Working to conserve the Thames

The success in conserving so many nature reserves along the Thames is the outcome of many people's hard work, and the best reward for these stalwarts is the appreciation shown by those who visit these places. Judging from the dedications on riverside benches, each reserve has been a favourite place for somebody. These dedications and the love of the river and its wildlife give us a sense of continuity in which the past flows into the present, and the present will run into the future.

Loddon Lake, where volunteers won an award in 2011

The wildlife of the river is a useful indicator of river health, habitat condition and water quality. Our job in looking after rivers is to keep the natural balance between the needs of people and of wildlife, and to maintain a sustainable and vibrant ecosystem so that the many species of life in the river can survive. In the 1950s the commonsense Countryside Code was established to help us all to respect, protect and enjoy our countryside. It applies to all parts of the countryside and was updated by Natural England in 2012. It can be found at www. naturalengland.org.uk.

The Environment Agency, with many non-government organisations such as the River Trusts and Wildlife Trusts, is taking the lead in restoring river wildlife habitats, as well as their work on flood defence, climate-change mitigation, pollution and the control of invasive species. The Port of London Authority also undertakes considerable river and habitat restoration in the tidal Thames and estuary creeks; and Thames21 engages the community in cleaning up the river environment and helping to raise public awareness and educating people about the benefits and value of rivers.

Volunteering with these key organisations helps to spread the load of work required and speeds up the progress that together we can make to improve our river resources. In the 'Get Involved' section on page 227 we have identified where you can participate in this rewarding work. We hope you will be inspired to get involved, to learn, and to play your part with the work that needs doing. Many different opportunities exist for people to participate with river activities – from weeding to planting native species; from sowing wildflowers to pruning; from tree planting to coppicing; from species monitoring to haymaking; from gardening

> *Many different opportunities exist for people to participate with river activities – from weeding to planting native species.*

National Trails volunteers at Little Meadow, Goring (reserve 61) and Grandpont (reserve 32)

Volunteers cut reeds and clear scrub at Trap Grounds Town Green (reserve 29)

to footpath maintenance.

One particular species that is puzzling scientists at present is the declining numbers of European eels. Eels were one of the first species to recolonise the Thames in the 1960s. It is thought that the recent fall in eel numbers may be due to the impact of climate change, changing sea currents, barriers formed by weirs and dams, disease and parasites. Eels are an important part of the estuary's food chain, feeding many of the larger birds on the Thames. Much work is now being done to remove in-river barriers that stop eels migrating upstream for food and to restore their natural European river habitats, and volunteers can help with eel monitoring in tributaries such as the Brent and Wandle. There are also opportunities for educating schoolchildren about the part that eels, as well as other rare species, play in the natural life of the river.

The Thames is also internationally famous for its vast numbers of mute white swans who reside there annually. Swan Upping is the traditional annual census of the mute swan population on the River Thames. It takes place in July each year, between Sunbury and Abingdon. This popular spectacle is an important part of the mute swan conservation programme in Britain and is managed by the Queen's Swan Warden. The warden collects data, assesses the health of young cygnets, and examines them for any injuries. Cygnets are extremely vulnerable at this early stage in their development and Swan Upping is an opportunity to help adults and cygnets that might otherwise go untreated. The practical conservation as well as educational values of these events was demonstrated during the 1980s when a serious decline in the swan population was halted by the replacement of lead fishing weights with a non-toxic equivalent.

The Royal Swan Uppers, who wear the scarlet uniform of Her Majesty the Queen, travel in traditional rowing skiffs with Swan Uppers from the Vintners' and Dyers' livery companies. Many local Thames Catchment schools are invited to meet the Swan Uppers on their journey upriver. The children can see cygnets at close quarters and ask questions about swans, the boats used, and the Queen's ownership of mute swans. The participation of schoolchildren is a positive element of Swan Upping and their enthusiasm for wildlife education and involvement is always to be encouraged.

With everyone joining in to help, we can ensure that the Thames continues to survive and flourish. And we can, through our combined actions, contribute to maintaining the river's natural function as a wildlife habitat and water source for many people and many species, for many years to come.

The Thames and its wildlife need continued care, and a repeat of past neglect must be avoided. The riverbanks need to be softened with vegetation and strengthened with natural materials, and all river organisations should have an environmental 'green' interest and a strong practical element in conserving the natural resources. The ideal should be that every part of the river and its adjacent land are managed to promote the growth of plants and the survival of animals, particularly those native to the Thames.

If you enjoy visiting the Thames wilderness, please consider joining some of the organisations that are committed to conservation of places on or near the Thames. You can expect a warm welcome, lots of interesting information to add to that given here, and opportunities to explore these places in depth. Often, you can take part in a particular event before joining and paying a subscription.

We have briefly mentioned voluntary work when describing some reserves, and this information is summarised in the table in the 'Get Involved' section that follows. The list is not comprehensive as there are other organisations – for example, fishing, rowing and sailing clubs – that take good care of their reaches of the river. So, if we work together, we can conserve the river that we love.

The swans believe they are the guardians of the Thames

Some volunteers prefer to take it easy!

Get Involved...

CONSERVATION VOLUNTEERING AND EDUCATION OPPORTUNITIES

Below is a list of the most well-known national organisations offering conservation volunteering and educational opportunities along the UK's rivers and canals.

Following that is a list of the specific volunteer organisations working in each section of the Thames as described in this book.

River Thames Society
www.riverthamessociety.org.uk

Thames Rivers Trust
www.thamesriverstrust.org.uk

The Rivers Trust
www.theriverstrust.org

The Wildlife Trusts
www.wildlifetrusts.org

Environment Agency
www.environment-agency.gov.uk

Friends of The Earth Trust
www.foe.co.uk

Canal and River Trust
www.canalrivertrust.org.uk

Angling Development Board
www.anglingtrust.net/adb

British Canoe Union
www.bcu.org.uk

Inland Waterways Association
www.waterways.org.uk

National Community Boats Association
www.national-cba.co.uk

Sustrans
www.sustrans.org.uk

Royal Society for the Protection of Birds
www.rspb.org.uk

Waterway Recovery Group
www.wrg.org.uk

National Waterways Museum
www.nwm.org.uk

Waterways Action Squad
www.waterwaysactionsquad.com

National Trust
www.nationaltrust.org.uk

British Trust for Conservation Volunteers
www.btcv.org.uk

Youth Hostel Association
www.yha.org.uk

Woodland Trust
www.woodlandtrust.org.uk

Ramblers Association
www.ramblers.org.uk

Soil Association
www.soilassociation.org

National Parks
www.nationalparks.gov.uk

Natural England
www.naturalengland.co.uk

Thames21
www.thames21.org.uk

Waterscape
www.waterscape.com

Do It
www.do-it.org.uk

Environment Trust for Richmond upon Thames
www.environmenttrust.co.uk

Wildfowl and Wetlands Trust
www.wwt.org.uk

Thames Path
www.nationaltrail.co.uk

The Waterways Trust
www.thewaterwaystrust.org.uk

The following are lists of the voluntary organisations specific to each chapter of the book.

CHAPTER 2 •• THE COTSWOLDS

Cotswold Water Park Trust
- www.waterpark.org/trust/volunteering_1.html
- ✉ info@waterpark.org
- ☎ CWP Trust office 01793 752 413

Wiltshire Wildlife Conservation Volunteers
- www.southwilts.com/site/Wiltshire-Wildlife-Conservation-Volunteers
- ✉ info@wwcv.co.uk
- ☎ 01793 694 680

Gloucestershire Wildlife Trust
- www.gloucestershirewildlifetrust.co.uk/how-you-can-help/volunteering
- ✉ info@gloucestershirewildlifetrust.co.uk
- ☎ 01452 383 333

CHAPTER 3 •• WEST OXFORDSHIRE TO NORTH OXFORD

Berks, Bucks & Oxon Wildlife Trust (BBOWT)
- www.bbowt.org.uk/how-you-can-help/volunteer
- ✉ volunteering@bbowt.org.uk
- ☎ 01865 788 309

Oxford Preservation Trust
- www.oxfordpreservation.org.uk/joinus
- ✉ volunteer@oxfordpreservation.org.uk
- ☎ 01865 242 918

The Friends of the Trap Grounds
- www.trap-grounds.org.uk
- ✉ volunteer@trap-grounds.org.uk
- ☎ 01865 511 307

Oxfordshire Conservation Volunteers
- www.ocv.org.uk
- ✉ enquiries@ocv.org.uk
- ☎ 07779 343 847

Roundhouse Lake

CHAPTER 4 ·· CENTRAL OXFORD TO ABINGDON

Oxfordshire Nature Conservation Forum
🖰 www.oncf.org.uk
✉ info@oncf.org.uk
☎ 01865 407 034

Berks, Bucks & Oxon Wildlife Trust (BBOWT)
🖰 www.bbowt.org.uk/how-you-can-help/volunteer
✉ volunteering@bbowt.org.uk
☎ 01865 788 309

Earth Trust
🖰 www.earthtrust.org.uk/supportus/volunteer.aspx
✉ support@earthtrust.org.uk
☎ 01865 409 426

The Friends of Aston's Eyot
🖰 www.friendsofastonseyot.org.uk
✉ info@friendsofastonseyot.org.uk

Oxford Preservation Trust
🖰 www.oxfordpreservation.org.uk/joinus
✉ volunteer@oxfordpreservation.org.uk
☎ 01865 242 918

Abingdon Green Gym, Barton Fields
🖰 www.abingdongreengym.org.uk/worksites/barton-fields

CHAPTER 5 ·· CULHAM TO TILEHURST

Beale Park
🖰 www.bealepark.co.uk/support_us/become_a_volunteer
✉ administration@bealepark.co.uk
☎ 08448 261 761

Berks, Bucks & Oxon Wildlife Trust (BBOWT)
🖰 www.bbowt.org.uk/how-you-can-help/volunteer
✉ volunteering@bbowt.org.uk
☎ 01865 788 309

Earth Trust
🖰 www.earthtrust.org.uk/supportus/volunteer.aspx
✉ support@earthtrust.org.uk
☎ 01865 409 426

Withymead Nature Reserve
🖰 www.withymead.co.uk
✉ info@withymead.co.uk
☎ 01491 872 265

Pangbourne Meadow

View from Cliveden

CHAPTER 6 ·· READING TO MAIDENHEAD

Berks, Bucks & Oxon Wildlife Trust (BBOWT)
🖱 www.bbowt.org.uk/how-you-can-help/volunteer
✉ volunteering@bbowt.org.uk
☎ 01865 788 309

River Thames Society
🖱 www.riverthamessociety.org.uk
✉ admin@riverthamessociety.org.uk
☎ 01491 612 456

Make Space for Life
🖱 www.makespaceforlife.org
✉ makespaceforlife@gmail.com

Cliveden National Trust Volunteers
🖱 www.nationaltrust.org.uk/cliveden
✉ cliveden@nationaltrust.org.uk
☎ 01628 605 069 (Estate Office)

CHAPTER 7 ·· BRAY TO CHERTSEY

Braywick Park and Nature Centre Volunteers
🖱 www.rbwm.gov.uk
✉ Online contact form on website
☎ 01628 683 800

Runnymede National Trust Volunteers
🖱 www.nationaltrust.org.uk/runnymede
✉ runnymede@nationaltrust.org.uk
☎ 01784 432 891

CHAPTER 8 ·· WEST LONDON

Friends of Bushy Park and Home Parks
- www.fbhp.org.uk
- chairman@fbhp.org.uk
- ☎ 0208 287 2748

Friends of Ham Lands
- www.fohl.org.uk
- info@fohl.org.uk

Thames Landscape Strategy
- www.thames-landscape-strategy.org.uk
- rebeccalaw@richmond.gov.uk
- ☎ 0208 940 0654

Environment Trust for Richmond upon Thames
- www.environmenttrust.co.uk/volunteering.html
- office@environmenttrust.co.uk
- ☎ 0208 891 5455

The Richmond Biodiversity Partnership
- www.richmond.gov.uk/biodiversity
- ☎ 0845 612 2660

Greenspace Information for Greater London
- www.gigl.org.uk
- mandy.rudd@gigl.org.uk
- ☎ 0207 803 4278

Friends of Kew Gardens
- www.kew.org
- info@kew.org
- ☎ 0208 332 5000

Wildfowl and Wetlands Trust
- www.wwt.org.uk
- enquiries@wwt.org.uk
- ☎ 01453 891 900

Thames21
- www.thames21.org.uk
- info@thames21.org.uk
- ☎ 0207 248 7171

Thames Anglers' Conservancy
- www.rivertac.org
- admin@rivertac.org

British Trust for Conservation Volunteers/ Conservation Volunteers/Do It (YouthNet)
- www.btcv.org.uk/www.do-it.org.uk
- ☎ 0207 250 5700

The Brent River & Canal Trust
- BrentRiverPark@live.co.uk
- ☎ 0208 930 4119

The Selbourne Society
- www.perivalewood.purplecloud.net
- contact@selbournesociety.org.uk
- ☎ 0208 840 3250

Thames Explorer Trust
- www.thames-explorer.org.uk
- info@thames-explorer.org.uk
- ☎ 0208 742 0057

In the tree canopy at Kew

Limehouse Dock

Herring gull at Crossness

CHAPTER 9 •• EAST LONDON

Mudchute Park and Farm
- 🖰 www.mudchute.org/support-us/volunteering
- ✉ farm@mudchute.org
- ☎ 0207 515 5901

Trust for Urban Ecology (TRUE)
- 🖰 www.urbanecology.org.uk/volunteering.html
- ✉ true@btcv.org.uk
- ☎ 0208 293 1904

Thames21
- 🖰 www.thames21.org.uk
- ✉ info@thames21.org.uk
- ☎ 0207 248 7171

Creekside Education Trust
- 🖰 www.creeksidecentre.org.uk/about-creekside/volunteering
- ✉ info@creeksidecentre.org.uk
- ☎ 0208 692 9922

Friends of Greenwich Park
- 🖰 www.friendsof greenwichpark.org.uk
- ✉ info@friendsofgreenwichpark.org.uk
- ☎ 0208 852 9540

Crossness Engines Trust
- 🖰 www.crossness.org.uk
- ✉ crossness@btconnect.com
- ☎ 0208 311 3711

Thames Anglers' Conservancy
- 🖰 www.rivertac.org
- ✉ admin@rivertac.org

CHAPTER 10 •• NORTH KENT

Royal Society for the Protection of Birds
- www.rspb.org.uk/volunteering
- ☎ 01767 680 551

RSPB Bexley Group
- www.bexleyrspb.org.uk
- ✉ stuartbans@hotmail.co.uk
- ☎ 0208 854 7251

Kent Wildlife Trust
- www.kentwildlifetrust.org.uk/volunteering
- ✉ info@kentwildlife.org.uk
- ☎ 01622 662 012

Medway Valley Countryside Partnership
- www.s400871350.initial-website.co.uk
- ✉ medwayvalley@kent.gov.uk
- ☎ 01622 683 695

CHAPTER 11 •• SOUTH ESSEX

Royal Society for the Protection of Birds – South Essex
- www.southendrspb.co.uk
- ☎ 01268 559 158

Essex Wildlife Trust and Thurrock Nature Reserve
- www.essexwt.org.uk/get_involved/volunteering
- ✉ admin@essexwt.org.uk
- ☎ 01621 862 960

Mucking Mudflats

Index

The end of the day on Port Meadow